Second Edition

Designing and Using

RUBRICS

for Reading and
Language Arts,
K–6

Second Edition

Designing and Using

RUBRICS

for Reading and Language Arts, K–6

Joan F. Groeber

CORWIN PRESS
A SAGE Publications Company
Thousand Oaks, CA 91320

For information:

Corwin Press
A Sage Publications Company
2455 Teller Road
Thousand Oaks, California 91320
www.corwinpress.com

Sage Publications Ltd
1 Oliver's Yard
55 City Road
London EC1Y 1SP
United Kingdom

Sage Publications India Pvt. Ltd.
B-42, Panchsheel Enclave
Post Box 4109
New Delhi 110 017 India

Printed in the United States of America on acid-free paper

Library of Congress Cataloging-in-Publication Data

Groeber, Joan F.
Designing and using rubrics for reading and language
arts, K-6 / Joan F. Groeber. — 2nd ed.
    p. cm.
Rev. ed. of: Designing rubrics for reading and language arts. 2003
Includes bibliographical references and index.
ISBN 1-4129-3785-X (cloth) — ISBN 1-4129-3786-8 (pbk.)
    1. Language arts—Ability testing—United States. 2. Reading—Ability testing—United States. 3. Competency based educational tests—United States. I. Groeber, Joan F. Designing rubrics for reading and language arts. II. Title.

LB1576.G78 2007
372.6—dc22   2006014860

06 07 08 09 10 10 9 8 7 6 5 4 3 2 1

Acquisitions editor:	Cathy Hernandez
Editorial assistant:	Charline Wu
Production editor:	Sanford Robinson
Copy editor:	Cheryl Duksta
Typesetter:	C&M Digitals (P) Ltd.
Cover designer:	Monique Hahn
Graphic Designer:	Lisa Miller
Indexer:	Kirsten Kite

Contents

Preface

In recent years, many educators have demonstrated genuine interest in exploring authentic learning opportunities for their students. As individual schools and entire districts seek ways to incorporate this approach into the existing curriculum, a major concern is identifying and implementing a form of student assessment tailored to this learning style. The most frequently discussed option is rubrics.

A rubric is a grid or chart that expresses requirements of a task by dividing them into a range of achievement levels. It is an assessment method that identifies specific steps within a multistep process (e.g., constructing a Web page), then defines levels of performance for each step from minimal to optimal expectations based on student age and grade level. Rubrics make an excellent assessment tool for authentic learning tasks because they can include all critical steps as well as levels of performance for each step (Burke, 2006). Authentic learning seeks to replicate real-life experience with tasks that mirror what occurs in the real world. Authentic learning introduces skills that often fall outside the existing curriculum; therefore, assessment of authentic learning tasks requires a new system of measuring student understanding. Rubric assessment is ideal for the multitask nature of authentic learning because it allows for evaluation of several elements at the same time. For example, students participating in a debate can be evaluated on debate content as well as acceptable behaviors related to that type of oral presentation, such as "no interrupting" or "respecting time limits."

Rubrics used to assess authentic learning provide students with a clear understanding of teacher expectations from the onset of the assignment. Rubrics can reduce or eliminate much of the subjectivity of assessment by clarifying for students the skills, knowledge, and behaviors they must demonstrate to attain a particular grade. When students know the teacher's expectations before beginning a performance task, they are able to assume greater responsibility for both learning and assessment. All students can identify the highest performance level and set goals for attaining that level.

Although rubrics can assess a wide variety of tasks, one of their more attractive features is an ability to evaluate the performance of students involved in activities specific to an individual classroom or school district. For example, a teacher may develop and implement a simulation activity for students in a middle school government class. The simulation may involve role playing, math computations, and debates as well as some written reflections about the experience. The teacher can design a rubric to cover each of these individual areas within the simulation, providing teacher and students with a more complete profile of overall performance. Instead of simply a letter or numerical grade, the rubric provides specific information about a student's strengths and weaknesses, a feature that helps students and teachers know the direction subsequent instruction should take.

A rubric allows teachers and districts to target areas of study specific to their district. For example, a school district may require students to demonstrate understanding of their state's government. A rubric can be designed to accommodate this situation. Students might participate in an authentic learning exercise, such as acting as state governor for a week. Teachers might evaluate this simulation on a number of levels, ranging from students' knowledge of the function of state government to the duties of the governor. By placing the district requirements on a rubric illustrating lowest to highest performance in each area, the teacher and students can see almost immediately those areas that require instruction and review.

In short, rubrics provide a comprehensive profile of student performance in highly readable results that offer teachers, administrators, parents, and students invaluable information for future planning. Using rubrics is a more complete assessment process than simply assigning overall letter grades because rubrics delineate all the tasks within a multitask procedure, and they identify criteria for mastery in each of these tasks.

HOW TO USE THIS BOOK

Designing and Using Rubrics for Reading and Language Arts, K–6 was written with a dual purpose. One goal is to provide teachers in all settings with rubrics to assess student literacy. To that end, this book contains samples of rubrics for each of the literacy areas tailored to specific grade levels—primary (K–3) and intermediate (4–6)—so teachers can track student achievement with a realistic scale. The presence of multiple grade levels allows teachers to see what their students should know in their present grade level as well as what teachers will expect of them as they progress through the school system.

Accompanying each sample rubric are guidelines for using the rubrics. These how-to pages offer sample assignments as well as acceptable responses for these assignments. Although teachers should begin their review of rubrics with the grade level they teach, they should not overlook the materials and information available at the other grade levels. They should peruse the other rubrics and how-to pages for alternative activity ideas and assessment options, which may be useful for differentiating assignments to meet individual student needs.

Benchmarks for each level are included, as well as suggested activities in many areas. Each sample rubric shows a specific grading scale (93–100 = A; 87–92 = B; 78–86 = C; 70–77 = D; < 70 = F). Criteria in the rubrics are typical of those found in state standards. The appendix contains a list of Web sites that offer information on standards across the United States, helpful information on rubrics, and other useful teacher-related Web sites.

In addition to providing time-saving, preconstructed rubrics, the other goal of this book is to provide teachers with a step-by-step guide to constructing their own rubrics for any classroom performance task.

The major revisions to the second edition are twofold. First, the material has been reorganized to better meet the needs of teachers. The chapter on designing rubrics has been updated and moved to the front of the book. Second, several new rubrics have been added to reflect the expanding field of literacy and language arts education. Included in the new edition are rubrics that address narrative writing, persuasive writing, six-trait writing, comprehension monitoring, the use of presentation software, and information literacy skills. In addition, the book has been refocused to target educators in primary and intermediate classroom settings. In this way, the book remains an essential resource for teachers in those grades and adds information and rubrics to meet the new challenges facing these educators.

This new edition is divided into eight chapters. Chapter 1 offers a general overview of rubrics and explains why they have become such a popular assessment instrument. This chapter gives a detailed account of how and when rubrics are most effectively used. Chapter 2 provides a clear description of how to construct rubrics and offers several sample rubrics as well as methods for altering samples and developing rubrics that can assess specific classroom assignments. Chapter 3 gives educators tools for assessing students' reading comprehension. Concrete examples of activities and rubrics use are found throughout this section. Chapter 4 focuses on assessing students' understanding of fictional story elements. Many times, readers are able to decode and comprehend fictional stories but fail to see a connection between various works of fiction and the importance of such elements as characterization and theme. Chapter 5 provides ways for teachers to assess different forms of student writing. The chapter includes rubrics for the writing process and six-trait writing, as well as rubrics for specific assignments, such as letters and greeting cards. These rubrics, like all of the samples provided in the book, can be adapted by teachers as needed. Chapter 6 covers oral language skills, including oral reports and presentations. This chapter allows educators to focus on helping students learn effective presentation skills. Chapter 7 explores the research process and offers sample rubrics that enable educators to help students learn the skills necessary to advance to formal research projects in higher grades. Sample rubrics examine if students are able to use such research tools as a dictionary and an atlas effectively. Chapter 8 includes assessment of students' ability to use classroom technology to convey information to others. Sample rubrics in this chapter focus on information literacy skills and the use of presentation software to construct and deliver multimedia presentations.

Finally, although the primary focus of this book is the language arts of reading, writing, listening, and speaking, the assessment rubrics are also useful for content-focused assignments. For example, teachers can use the research rubrics when teaching social studies, the debate rubrics for science tasks, and the presentation rubrics for mathematics assignments.

Publisher's Acknowledgments

Corwin Press gratefully acknowledges the contributions of the following reviewers:

Eileen E. Atwood, Fifth-Grade Teacher
Westridge Elementary School, Woodbridge, VA

Barbara A. Bradley, Assistant Professor of Teaching and Leadership
University of Kansas, Lawrence, KS

Tracy Taylor Callard, Fifth-Grade Teacher
Wichita Collegiate School, Wichita, KS

Alexis Ludewig, Third-Grade Teacher
St. Germain Elementary School, St. Germain, WI

About the Author

 **Joan F. Groeber** is an independent consultant and lecturer in the field of literacy and assessment. She is a visiting literacy instructor in the College of Education at Wright State University in Dayton, Ohio. Joan has published eight books and more than 30 articles on literacy and assessment tools, classroom management strategies, and self-evaluation for educators from kindergarten to the college level. Her most recent book, *The Dogtors Partnership: Listening to Buffy's Eyes,* deals with animal-assisted therapy and chronicles her journey into this fascinating field with her partner Duke, a golden retriever.

Dedication

To those individuals in my life who have encouraged me to live, think, and dream outside the world of "what is" and remain steadfast in their loyalty and support as I venture into the universe of "what could be."

Rubrics—A General Overview

Suzanne, a first-year teacher, is committed to designing lessons that promote authentic learning for her students. In developing these activities, Suzanne is experiencing difficulty finding a way to assess student understanding of the concepts she presents in class. She is also struggling with assigning letter or numerical grades that reflect performance.

RUBRICS TO ASSESS AUTHENTIC LEARNING

Not only beginning educators face Suzanne's problems. As all educators explore new ways of instructing students, they must also identify methods for evaluating students' grasp of concepts and ideas. The growing interest in authentic learning challenges teachers and administrators to examine current evaluation strategies. Carlson (2002) explained that *authentic learning* means "learning that uses real world problems and projects and that allows students to explore and discuss the problems in ways that are relevant to them." The authentic-learning classroom is a learner-centered environment in which students are encouraged to become active learners. The tasks in an authentic-learning classroom are relevant to students' real-life experiences. Many grading practices now in use are unsuitable for recording student performance on authentic-learning tasks. Authentic learning uses collaborative effort, problem-solving opportunities, and dialogue with informed sources to create a real-life learning situation. For example, in an authentic-learning unit on weather, students would use some of the same tools used by a meteorologist, such as a rain gauge and barometer. A simple letter or numerical grade used in traditional assessment practices does not provide enough information for such tasks. Using rubrics, the teacher can establish a set of performance guidelines ranging from inadequate to mastered, providing students with a clear understanding of expectations from the onset of an instructional activity (Arter & McTighe, 2000).

In addition to offering clear standards to students participating in authentic-learning activities, rubrics, with their multitask evaluation, are well suited to a process approach to learning because teachers can use them to evaluate performance for many phases within a single experience (O'Neil, 1996). For example, Chapter 5 describes the five-step writing process. Teachers can use a single rubric to assess student performance during each step of the five-step process.

WHAT IS A RUBRIC?

A rubric is a flexible assessment tool. A rubric allows teachers to make more precise and useful measurements because, unlike conventional grading methods in the areas of language arts and reading, the rubric lists criteria necessary to attain graduated levels of mastery. In addition, using a rubric gives teachers the ability to set up criteria for each phase of an activity. For example, when evaluating an oral presentation, the teacher assigns a grade based on a number of factors, including vocal projection, content, nonverbal language, and the ability to capture and maintain audience attention. The teacher can construct the rubric to list each of these criteria with varying levels of performance, ranging from, for example, "fails to make eye contact" to "uses facial gestures to emphasize remarks" under the nonverbal language area.

Rubrics can be tailored to meet the individual needs of a teacher or a school district, but all rubrics contain certain elements. Each rubric contains an objective, or stated skill, behavior, or attitude, such as comprehension of a passage of expository writing or delivery of an oral report. Objectives may contain a number of components. Taking again the example of an oral report, the teacher must look at a number of factors, including vocal projection and clarity, quality of content, nonverbal language, and audience appeal. On a rubric, these areas would appear in a list in a random or specific (alphabetical or order of importance) sequence.

The most common arrangement for a rubric is a grid. The vertical axis lists the skills, behaviors, and attitudes required for successful completion of the task. For example, on the rubric evaluating oral presentations, the list might include the general areas of quality of content, vocal projection and clarity, nonverbal language, and audience appeal.

The rubric also includes more detailed features that would enhance or detract from a student's grade. For example, each rubric could list specific elements that fall within these areas of evaluation. For example, in the area of vocal projection and clarity, the ideal includes qualities such as "uses suitable volume," "enunciates clearly," and "exhibits no halting and repetition of words." Students who achieve these criteria receive a grade that reflects mastery in this area.

Even though all the items appear within one heading in both sample rubrics, the rubrics allow teachers to evaluate each item. Each rubric contains a range, such as 1 to 4 points. The range of achievement on a rubric enables evaluators to gauge student performance against learning standards, rather than simply calling a performance "right" or "wrong." The point values appear at the top of each column, which allows teachers to add them easily to arrive at a final grade. Assigning 0 points is a feasible option: If the student's work demonstrates no evidence of the criterion, the student receives no credit. Because a simpler rubric is more appropriate at the primary level, the primary-level rubrics in this book have a range of 0 to 2 points.

Focus on the category vocal projection and clarity, which evaluates three elements. If none of these elements could be considered present in a student's oral presentation, the rubric score would be no credit, or 0. If the student makes an attempt to achieve at least two elements under vocal projection and clarity but falls short in his or her efforts, the score would be 1 point to indicate an incomplete attempt. If the student achieves one of the three stated criteria completely, the score would be 2 points; if the student achieves two of the criteria completely, the score would be 3 points, and so on. Thinking of the rubric range as it relates to standards may be helpful. A score of 1 point is low: The student has not met the standards. Scores of 2 or 3 points indicate that the student has met some portion of the overall standard, and a score of 4 points indicates the student has met the standards. These rubric scores make up the eventual letter grade (an explanation of this conversion appears later in this chapter in the section titled "Converting Rubric Scores"). This feature of the rubric allows educators to pinpoint specific areas of strength or weakness, providing the student with more useful feedback for future presentations than a simple letter grade (A, B, C, etc.) or assigned percentage (96%, 85%, etc.). Teachers can show students how they convert the presence of these criteria to a letter or number grade.

On many rubrics, certain elements carry more weight than others (spelling is not as critical in a written report as content), and the numerical ranges help teachers and students make that distinction. Some educators refer to rubrics with this feature as weighted rubrics. All the rubrics in this book are weighted; in other words, all assign a larger point value to the most important elements of the lesson.

Weighted rubrics are one way to establish degrees of proficiency on the rubric. For example, rubrics assessing research writing have one criterion that covers the article's bibliography. Students receive no points, of course, if no bibliography is present, but if their bibliography contains only books, they might receive only 1 point; a multimedia bibliography that includes journal articles, Web sites, and videos related to the unit topic might receive 4 points. The scope of the bibliography (all book references, all Internet references, a mix of print, Internet, and video references) influences the grade. In short, a solely literature-based bibliography no longer represents the highest degree of competency or "correctness." Because the teacher distributes the rubrics at the start of the research unit, students are aware of this expectation before they begin their research. Once students have seen a completed rubric, teachers can actively involve them in the construction of rubrics. This helps students develop a clearer understanding of the types of criteria teachers take into consideration when assessing assignments. Educators in a wide variety of settings have found that the basic features of objective, range, and degree make the rubric a practical, adaptable assessment tool.

WHY USE RUBRICS?

Because using rubrics may require additional planning in an educator's already time-challenged schedule, one might question why this assessment method is worth the extra effort. The most obvious reason is the rubric's unique capacity to quantify student performance in a relatively objective manner.

Rubrics enable teachers to establish a set of criteria for completion of specified tasks, and rubrics give students the opportunity to see which skills and behaviors are expected for mastery of each task (Arter & McTighe, 2000). For these reasons, teachers must have the rubric ready before they make the assignment, and students need to see the rubric before they undertake the assignment. Seeing the rubric at the beginning of an activity allows students to be fully aware of what the teacher expects of them in the assignment and helps students become actively involved in their learning.

When educators in a particular grade level, school, or district reach a consensus about performance standards for specific tasks, the rubric's benefits become even more apparent. Having a consistent measurement of the standards set by a school district—say, 90% on a particular skill to be considered proficient—benefits teachers and students. For example, when students move from school to school, a universal form of measurement makes it easier to ease the new students into the classroom.

Rubrics provide students and their parents and guardians with a clear idea of expectations, eliminating confusion and frustration throughout all phases of the learning experience. Knowing what teachers expect reduces students' anxieties as they approach an assigned task. Whether or not they are able to attain mastery of all task-related components, students have an opportunity to examine the expected level of competency and to set goals. With rubrics, students can easily identify their weakest areas and place greater concentration and effort on improving them.

As educators such as the first-year teacher in the scenario at the beginning of this chapter attempt to involve students in more authentic learning, they must identify methods for assessing understanding. They must determine student achievement in a different way because the assignments often fall outside the category of traditional direct instruction (games, simulations, workshops). The flexibility and increased detail of the rubric make it an obvious choice for assessment purposes.

At the completion of an activity, teachers can use the information the completed rubric provides in a number of ways. The organization of the rubric offers easy identification of patterns that may suggest the need for additional instruction. For example, if all or most students scored low on the vocal projection and clarity component of an oral presentation rubric, educators may find it helpful to work with students in small or large groups in an alternate venue, such as the gym or cafeteria, to strengthen vocal projection. If an individual student consistently scored low on a specific area of the rubric, the teacher may use this information to prepare additional instruction for that student. Finally, if all students received a low score on an element, it may indicate inadequate preparation or lack of instruction in that area.

Mining the information on an assessment rubric provides teachers with opportunities to encourage students to develop their specific strengths (audience appeal) while offering suggestions on how to target areas of weakness (vocal projection and clarity) with tangible strategies. For example, teachers might suggest that, when students practice their presentation, they stand at the back of a room and speak loud enough to be heard by a classmate at the opposite side of the room.

RUBRICS VERSUS CHECKLISTS

Checklists may be regarded as the forerunner of the rubric, even though both assessment instruments remain in use. Like the rubric, the checklist contains criteria necessary for mastery of a specific task. Absence of one or more of the stated criteria can detract from a student's overall grade on a particular activity. The checklist and the rubric provide students with a clear idea of educator expectations.

Although both assessment tools offer students more information than a letter or numerical grade, the rubric takes the criteria list one step farther by associating stated performance standards with graduated levels of mastery. For example, a checklist might remind students that they must edit written reports for punctuation errors; however, a rubric states the same objective with graduated levels of mastery: 0–1 errors = 4 points, 2–4 errors = 3 points, and so on. This additional information allows educators to distinguish between minor lapses in punctuation (2 or 3 punctuation errors) and a significant lack of understanding of correct punctuation (8 to 10 errors). This feature of the rubric makes it a more objective evaluation instrument than the checklist, where educator discrimination determines whether students receive full credit for correcting punctuation errors. In a weighted rubric, of course, teachers would assign a lower value ($n \times 1$) to punctuation and give more points ($n \times 4$) to the content and organization of a composition so that the number of punctuation errors does not decrease the grades of good but careless writers.

Although the comprehensive nature of the rubric offers students and educators more information regarding performance on specific tasks, the checklist remains a useful assessment instrument, particularly when teachers can evaluate the stated objective with a yes-or-no response to questions such as "Does the written report contain a title?"

WHEN TO USE RUBRICS

A rubric is appropriate in all learning situations. Teachers can use it to evaluate oral and written assignments and individual and group presentations. Although sometimes regarded largely as an assessment instrument, teachers should make rubrics available to students during the early phases of the lesson or unit.

It is essential that educators construct and distribute the assessment rubric for a specific task before designing and executing related activities for three important reasons: to guide lesson planning, to make students aware of lesson objectives and teacher expectations, and to help students assume responsibility for their learning. Having the rubric at the onset of a unit, lesson, or activity assists in lesson planning because it gives teachers the opportunity to reflect on their expectations and make certain that students have ample instruction and opportunities for growth in those areas. For example, if a rubric on debating concentrates on students' ability to stay focused on the topic regardless of the nature of opponents' comments, the teacher must plan instructional time to emphasize this skill. The additional time invested in this area alerts students to its importance in their preparation as debaters.

Second, showing and discussing rubrics with students at the start of a lesson or assignment alerts students to the areas the teacher considers most important for mastery of the unit or task and gives students insight into specific goals the teacher has set for activities. Students can begin to think about these expectations and look for ways to meet the criteria in the most effective manner. Rather than attempting to absorb every piece of information the teacher presents, students are able to rank the information's importance, investing more time and energy in those areas deemed essential to mastery of a specific task. They have time to ask questions and focus their efforts on those areas where they are weakest. For example, if a rubric for oral presentation lists "makes eye contact with audience" or "uses a strong opening statement" as the most essential factors, students can focus their primary attention on those areas of their presentation. Because its purpose is to convey a set of standards for a particular task, presenting the rubric at or near the completion of the task diminishes its function as an organizational tool and guiding force in students' preparation and execution of various tasks.

Finally, when students have an opportunity to view an assessment rubric at the onset of a lesson or assignment, they gain a sense of control over their learning; therefore, distributing rubrics before an assignment helps students become more actively involved in their learning. With the expectations in hand before they begin an assignment, students must assume responsibility for meeting the expectations. There can be no claims of "I didn't know that's what you wanted" or "You never said we had to do that." Teachers who use rubrics can effectively transfer responsibility for learning to students. This active involvement in their own learning also promotes an increased interest on the part of students.

To help students understand this form of assessment, students should have the opportunity to assign rubric scores. They might practice assigning scores in workshop settings when reading their peers' essays, they might complete them for their peers giving oral presentations, and so on. They might also create their own rubrics.

Student-Created Rubrics

One of the most effective ways teachers can introduce rubrics in the classroom is to engage students in actively constructing rubrics. Stiggins (2004) explained that involving students in developing classroom assessments helps students gain a clear understanding of how their work will be judged. Participating in the development of rubrics helps students begin to assume responsibility for their own learning by building understanding of the criteria teachers consider in compiling an overall grade. In addition, partnering with the teacher in deciding what constitutes an ideal presentation, debate, or report increases student understanding of the evaluation process.

CONVERTING RUBRIC SCORES

At present, most school districts continue to use some form of letter or numerical grading system. For the rubric to be an effective assessment tool, a widely accepted method of converting its information to this grading system must exist. Assigning a particular weight (in numbers) to specific components of a task provides educators with the basis for converting rubric points into more traditional letter or numerical grades.

The most direct method of converting rubric scores is with a key at the bottom of the rubric that links student performance to a letter grade. To arrive at values for a letter grade of A, B, C, and so on, one simply divides the number of points earned by the total number of points available. For example, earning 19 points out of a possible 20 points yields a score of 95%, which the majority of grading standards would consider a grade of A. A score of 18 out of 20 yields 90%. Depending on the grade scale a school system uses, this grade might be considered an A (in a 90–100 classification) or a B (in a 93–100 classification). When creating a rubric, teachers should calculate the percentages for each possibility and list the results in a key somewhere on the rubric.

Teachers assign a specified number of points for each criterion listed under each objective on a rubric They then combine these individual numbers to report a total score on the task. Because quality of content should be considered more critical than speaking volume on an oral report, criteria under the *quality-of-content* objective would be worth more points than the criteria under the vocal-projection-and-clarity objective. Students who present an oral report of little or no substance would receive a much lower grade than a student whose report contains high-quality content but who needs to improve in the area of vocal projection. This type of weighted evaluation provides students with clear expectations concerning which aspects of their report preparation and presentation are most important.

AN EFFECTIVE ASSESSMENT TOOL AND MORE

The rubric is much more than an effective tool for measuring performance tasks. It is also an instructional tool that enables teachers to clarify specific components of a task at the onset of a lesson or assignment, to indicate which parts of the task are most important, and to explain what will be judged an acceptable performance on the various components of the task.

The following chapters provide sample rubrics for a wide variety of learning experiences, beginning with the assessment of reading comprehension. Because a clear understanding of the reading process and the selection and use of quality literature are essential components in any curriculum, it is important to invest some time and effort in reviewing these areas in detail. For this reason, Chapters 3 and 4 include an in-depth look at the reading process and the elements of story structure, including additional suggestions for class discussion topics and activities. These two chapters lay the foundation for rubric assessment in reading and the language arts, and the remaining chapters on writing, listening, speaking, research, and technology build on this foundation. Chapters 5 through 8 contain numerous self-explanatory rubrics and activities and require only minimal introduction and explanation. It is important to note that all of the rubrics provided in this book are intended to offer educators practical guidelines and can be modified to maximize their effectiveness in individual classrooms.

Begin by reviewing the rubrics and the accompanying information for the grade level you teach, but do not overlook the information and rubrics for the other levels. Because students have varying learning needs, the rubrics for other grade levels might be useful when planning for differentiated assignments and assessment options.

Constructing Rubrics

2

Intermediate unit teachers Nick and Judy are delighted with a districtwide decision to use rubrics in the student assessment process. Receiving a packet containing several sample rubrics, Nick expresses concern that none of the samples fits a special environmental awareness unit he conducts each year with his fifth-grade class. Judy suggests a miniworkshop for teachers interested in constructing their own rubrics. She adds that she and her colleagues could use many of the strategies developed for such a program to help students create rubrics as a way of comprehending the process and purpose of the rubric. The principal agrees and contacts the university to schedule a workshop with one of the College of Education professors.

TEACHER-CREATED RUBRICS

Although this book contains rubrics for many areas of language arts, educators may assess a particular activity in their curriculum more effectively with their own teacher-created rubric. For this reason, teachers should understand how to create their own rubrics. It's critical to point out that the rubrics in this book are meant to serve as a guideline for teachers to use when creating their own rubrics or modifying the samples found in this book. Even if educators find it unnecessary to use a language arts rubric beyond those in this book, they should know how to construct a rubric.

Creating personalized rubrics allows teachers to tailor assessment to the individual needs of their students and the school's curriculum. The discussion of rubric construction in this chapter begins with a detailed description of all that rubric construction involves and includes examples of rubrics under construction. The discussion ends with a step-by-step summary. This chapter also discusses ways to involve students more fully in rubrics assessment.

UNDERSTANDING RUBRIC CONSTRUCTION

A number of variations in rubric construction enable educators to tailor this assessment tool to the individual needs of the learners in their classroom. There are, however, some basic constants for rubric construction. One common element of a rubric is a goal. The goal represents the objective being measured and assessed by the rubric. Whether a goal is part of a larger exercise or simply one task, educators know what is being evaluated and clearly convey this information to students. Another common element is the range or set of guidelines that informs students of expectations regarding a particular objective. For example, if an intermediate-level teacher is evaluating student achievement on a collaborative report, one component may be "fair distribution of tasks," with points being added or deducted based on the group's ability to manage tasks equitably. The highest level of the rubric might read "each group member invests equal time," whereas the lowest level might read "one student completes majority of tasks." These guidelines let students know the different levels of performance. Finally, the component of a standard or level of mastery lets students know exactly which criteria must be met to earn the highest (or lowest) grade on their assignment. These components should be clearly identified in all rubrics so that students are able to rely on their presence to chart their own progress.

CONSTRUCTING A RUBRIC

The first step in constructing a rubric is to identify a particular skill, behavior, or attitude to evaluate. This skill, behavior, or attitude should not be too specific ("recognizes sound of /ch/ digraph") or too broad ("reading") in nature. A good example might be the rubric titled "Oral Presentation—Debate." Every objective listed on the rubric must relate to the assessment of student performance during an oral debate.

As this book illustrates, the most common arrangement for a rubric is a grid. On the vertical axis, list the skills, behaviors, and attitudes of a master debater. Reflect on general areas, such as quality of content, vocal projection and clarity, knowledge of subject matter, and professional attitude.

Criteria					
Quality of content					
Vocal projection and clarity					
Knowledge of subject matter					
Professional attitude					

The next step involves focusing on each of the areas to evaluate, delineating (as in the "Oral Presentation—Debate" rubric) exactly which skills a master debater possesses. For example, the following elements are essential to the objective "professional attitude": "adheres to specified time limits," "does not interrupt opponent," and "listens attentively to opponent." Because no individual is perfect and even seasoned debaters experience occasional lapses, the rubric identifies several levels of proficiency.

Before evaluating student performance on a task, educators must examine the task, dissecting its components to determine which parts are more essential to an understanding of the task. For example, ability to proofread a written assignment for punctuation and capitalization errors is an essential step in the writing process, but the ability to compose a cohesive and coherent sentence is more crucial to the success of the writing task. Weighted rubrics permit the evaluator to assign more importance or weight to various aspects of a single task.

The arrangement of these elements in a weighted rubric is the evaluator's choice. One method lists the criteria in the first column, as shown in the following rubric, then delineates in subsequent columns how many criteria students must meet to attain the specific number of points identified in the column heading (students must meet all three criteria to earn 4 points, they must meet two criteria to earn 3 points, etc.).

Criteria	4	3	2	1	Total Points
Quality of content					
Vocal projection and clarity					
Knowledge of subject matter					
Professional attitude • adheres to specified time limits • does not interrupt opponent • listens attentively to opponent	3 complete elements present	2 complete elements present	1 complete element present	Evidence of 2+ incomplete elements present	

Another approach lists the objective in the first column, as shown in the following variation of the debate rubric and the remaining columns of the rubric illustrate higher standards of performance. Either format is suitable for most tasks. The first method notes whether a certain behavior is present or absent, and the second method illustrates specifically what merits 4 points, 3 points, and so on.

Criteria	4	3	2	1	Total Points
Quality of content					
Vocal projection and clarity					
Knowledge of subject matter					
Professional attitude	Adheres to all debating rules	Treats opponent respectfully	Adheres to specified time limits	Displays some inappropriate behaviors	

There is some discussion about the order of degrees of proficiency on the rubric. Some educators believe that putting the minimum standards first encourages students to set their goals too low and settle for a mediocre performance. Other educators believe that putting the most difficult standards first discourages less proficient students. Again, the choice is at the discretion of the educator/administrator.

The scoring column allows educators to emphasize the relative importance of the various criteria of an assignment. For example, in the Oral Presentation–Debate example, an educator may decide that demonstrating a professional attitude, a trait that will likely transfer into other areas of students' work, is of greater importance than knowledge of subject matter. Although each criterion listed on a rubric contributes to the overall grade, educators may wish to highlight the greater importance of a criterion by increasing the possible points that may earned for each level attained as shown in the following rubric.

Criteria	4	3	2	1	Total Points
Quality of content					_____ × 3 = _____ points
Vocal projection and clarity					_____ × 3 = _____ points
Knowledge of subject matter					_____ × 3 = _____points
Professional attitude					_____ × 4 = _____ points

Finally, most assessment rubrics have a conversion chart or key, explaining how to convert the rubric points to numerical or letter grades. To create this key, divide the total number of points assessed by the total number of points possible. For example, if the total number of points for an assignment is 52 and the student's score is 39, divide 39 by 52 for a result of .75, which you then convert to 75%. Convert this percentage to the grade scale of the school or district (93–100 = A, 85–92 = B, 77–84 = C, 70–76 = D, etc.). This final step enables educators to quantify the information contained on an assessment rubric as a concrete evaluation of student performance on a wide variety of tasks.

Step-by-Step Overview of Rubric Construction

1. Identify the task (written report) or behavior (listening to a guest speaker) you wish to assess. Rubrics are most effective when ranking extended performance tasks (Gronlund, 1998) or those containing a number of objectives.

2. Reflect on the task. Identify its components. If the task requires students to create a class newsletter, they must demonstrate proficiency in areas such as the use of desktop publishing software and page layout features in addition to grammar and spelling.

3. Consider how to list the objectives for assessment. You might list objectives with several criteria under a single heading, resulting in a numerical grade based on the number of elements present in a student's work. Alternatively, you might list the objectives with graduated levels of mastery paired with each number on the scale.

4. Decide on the importance and value of each task component in determining the final score. In the example of a class newsletter, should spelling and grammar have the same weight as page layout? Individual teachers can make these decisions, or the decisions can be a consensus among unit team members. After you establish the criteria and scale, it is important to inform students that you will pay greater attention to certain areas during the assessment process.

5. Assign point values (1, 2, 3, 4) for each objective. Present these numbers alone or in conjunction with an appropriate statement (1—Title present but inappropriate; 4—Creative, relevant title).

6. Indicate how you will convert these scores to a letter or number grade. You might use traditional grading standards (93–100% = A, 85–92% = B, 78–84% = C, etc.) and express them by listing the actual totals on the rubric (15–18 = A, 12–14 = B, etc.).

STUDENT-CREATED RUBRICS

One of the most effective ways to help students understand the rubric assessment process is to allow them to create a rubric. Select a fun activity, such as a birthday party, field trip, or school dance, and with students brainstorm a list of related components. For example, elements related to a field trip might be means of conveyance, destination, food, and chaperones. Have students complete the rubric with the range of most and least desired choices in these areas. An example of a student-created rubric follows.

Participating in this exercise prepares students to construct genuine assessment rubrics. Begin by identifying a cooperative group task (oral report, puppet show), and, as a class, brainstorm the profile of an ideal outcome for the assignment, focusing on various objectives of the project. These ideas make up the highest score on the rubric. Encourage students to participate in this process. In addition to giving students a sense of involvement in their own assessment, educators can determine, by level and variety of student response, if the task is too far above or below students' ability. Once an ideal is established, educators can, with or without the aid of students, add less ideal versions of each objective to fill in the rubric.

When the cooperative group activity is complete, have students complete a rubric for each of their group members. Having students complete the rubric helps them understand the requirements the rubric describes, ensures their active involvement in both the activity and the assessment, and puts responsibility on scoring well on them because they helped create the rubric.

RUBRIC FOR ASSESSING A FIELD TRIP

Criteria	4 Can we stay all year?	3 Can we stay all day?	2 Sure beats P.E. class!	1 Let's stay in class.	Total Points
Getting there	Stretch limo with chauffeur	4 × 4s off-road scrambling	Soccer mom vans	Big, yellow school bus	____ × 3 = ____ points
Destination	Amusement park	Movie theater	Planetarium	School playground	____ × 4 = ____ points
Food	Deluxe catered meal	Favorite pizza place	Favorite fast food restaurant	Brown bag PB&J with chips	____ × 4 = ____ points
Chaperones	Favorite male and female celebrities	Favorite teachers	Room parents	Neighborhood bullies	____ × 4 = ____ points

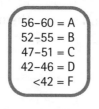

56–60 = A
52–55 = B
47–51 = C
42–46 = D
<42 = F

Total score ____/60 = ____

Many educators are familiar with the following Chinese proverb:

Tell me, I forget

Show me, I remember

Involve me, I understand.

By completing the rubric, students have a clearer understanding of what is involved when the teacher assesses them. Although it is likely that some students will still complain about their final grade, many more students will be able to see the connection between this exercise and how the teacher sets up a rubric to assess their performances. This activity also shows students that there is not always a pass-fail element to grades, and certain elements are more important than others and are weighted accordingly. Time spent engaging in this activity saves time later when teachers try to help students and their parents understand why students received a certain grade on an assignment.

STUDENT CHECKLISTS

Another way to help students understand the rubric and gauge their progress toward achievement of the required rubric elements is to provide them with a checklist to accompany the rubric. The checklist helps students see at a glance the areas they need to work on to complete a task successfully. Many of the tasks on the assessment rubric might be listed as smaller, more specific tasks on the checklist. (If the rubric contains an element regarding organization of ideas, a checklist might divide that task into two or more areas, such as "Do my ideas flow in an orderly sequence?" "Did I include only main ideas with no details?"). This enables students to see which elements go into the final product of a well-organized report as illustrated on the autobiography checklist that follows.

AUTOBIOGRAPHY CHECKLIST

Task	Yes	No
Cover design • Does my cover contain words and pictures or photos? • Does my cover relate to the contents of my autobiography? • Does my cover show some of my favorite things?		
Sequence • Do I tell my life story in order from when I was born to now? • Do I include big events that happened in my life?		

Task	Yes	No
• Do I get readers excited about reading the big events by using words that will make them curious about what comes next?		
Content • Do I use too many/too few pictures or photos? • Do I include captions to explain the pictures or photos? • Do the pictures or photos explain who I am?		

THE FUTURE OF RUBRICS

Although the use of rubrics in education will, in all likelihood, keep evolving, the value of rubric assessment will continue to be based on the rubric's ability to address individual assignments and be adapted for those assignments as needed. The weighted rubric with its graduated criteria scale will always be welcome in a classroom or school district where teachers are exploring authentic learning experiences and embracing less traditional methods of recording individual student growth and levels of understanding.

Using Rubrics to Assess Reading Comprehension

3

> Robert, a veteran educator, returned recently from a conference covering a number of assessment tools, including rubrics, and is eager to apply this information in his language arts classes. As Robert begins to construct rubrics for reading assessment, he realizes that because students must use different strategies to deal with different types of printed materials his rubrics for assessing their performance with each type of material must reflect these differences.

EXAMINING THE COMPONENTS OF READING COMPREHENSION

Most readers are introduced to printed material in the form of fiction such as bedtime stories and nursery rhymes. Exposure to nonfiction comes later through magazine articles and school textbooks. That most readers are introduced to fiction first is often regarded as one reason most readers prefer stories to nonfiction. But, more likely, readers gravitate to fiction because they share a certain amount of prior knowledge, an essential component for comprehension, with the story characters. In contrast, comprehension of nonfiction texts often requires some knowledge of the specialized vocabulary related to the topic as well as the ability to read and comprehend information contained in graphs and charts. The organization of nonfiction texts generally differs from fiction in its use of such text structures as description, sequence, comparison, cause and effect, or problem and solution. These differences in text structure and organization may account for the difference in reader comprehension of fiction and nonfiction texts. As a result, readers who are able to understand fictional material at a grade or ability level above their own may lack the skills necessary to read and interpret information found on a chart or graph, a deficit that affects their level of comprehension of nonfiction.

Using different rubrics for assessing student comprehension of various reading materials provides educators with a more detailed analysis of students' reading strengths and weaknesses. This information can prove invaluable in designing and executing reinforcement activities that target specific types of printed matter, such as charts and graphs.

READING FICTION

Fiction, through which most readers are introduced to the world of literature, is often relegated to a less critical position in many school curricula. The main reason cited for the shift in emphasis from use of fiction primarily in the early grades of school to nonfiction as students enter intermediate grades is the growing amount of factual information students must read within the limited time allotted for readers' formal education.

However, the shift in emphasis does not diminish the value of reading fiction. Contemporary fiction teaches the values, customs, and practices of a culture, and historical fiction offers a glimpse of these areas in another time period. Fantasy and science fiction nurture the imagination. The conflicts (man vs. self, man vs. man, man vs. nature, man vs. society) that fiction explores are the same as those found in the real world. Whether characters live on a remote prairie outpost or aboard a futuristic space station, readers experience their struggles vicariously, gaining insights for tackling problems in their own lives.

Fiction comes in a variety of categories to engage the imagination and suit the tastes of every reader:

- Contemporary, or realistic, fiction refers to fiction set in the present day. Examples of this genre include Katherine Paterson's *Bridge to Terabithia* and Beverly Cleary's *Dear Mr. Henshaw*.

- Historical fiction refers to fictional stories set in the past. Examples of this genre include Patricia MacLachlan's *Sarah, Plain and Tall*, and Laura Ingalls Wilder's *Little House in the Big Woods*.

- Fantasy or science fiction represents a literary form that extends the suspension of disbelief readers accept in literature to include such events as time travel, shape shifting, and talking animals while still pursuing answers to the universal questions of good versus evil and the meaning of life and death. Examples of fantasy include E. B. White's *Charlotte's Web*, Nancy Bond's *A String in the Harp*, Madeline L'Engle's *A Wrinkle in Time*, and J. K. Rowling's *Harry Potter and the Sorcerer's Stone*. Science fiction examples include Jill Paton Walsh's *The Green Book* and Jules Verne's *20,000 Leagues Under the Sea*.

- Folktales, legends, and myths are tales born of the oral tradition and contain simple, often didactic messages of how humans should conduct themselves. Examples include the tales of the brothers Grimm and Aesop's fables.

How to Use the
FICTION Rubric
at the Primary Level

Introduce the Rubric

Distribute and briefly discuss the rubric with students before they read the novel or short story. Explain that you will base the assessment on students' recognition of story classification, their ability to recount the story with emphasis on significant details, and their understanding of story conflict and theme. Ask students to keep these areas in mind as they read the book or short story.

Once students complete the reading, discuss the rubric elements thoroughly, making sure students understand your expectations and know that to receive full credit they must meet the objectives listed.

Make the Assignment

Introduce the story by examining the cover illustration and discussing the title with students. This activity helps young readers begin to think about the type of story they will read. Read the story aloud or, in the case of more mature readers, allow students to read the story silently.

Assess Student Understanding

Classification

- identifies story type
- recognizes story mood (happy, sad)

Early readers may not know the terms *fantasy, historical fiction,* or *science fiction,* but they should be able to identify some elements that distinguish the various genres. For example, readers should be able to recognize whether the story is set in the past, present, or future or in an imaginary world. Give each student four different-colored index cards. Then, after they read the story, have students hold up the colored card that designates whether the story is set in the present (blue), past (red), or future (yellow) or in an imaginary world (green). To prevent students from watching the cards of classmates, have students close their eyes or lay their heads on their desks while "voting." Conduct a similar activity to determine the mood of the story (happy, sad) with cards printed with happy or sad faces.

FICTION

Task: Student will read and respond to a work of fiction.

Goal/Standard: Demonstrate understanding through oral or written response

Criteria	2	1	0	Total Points
Classification • identifies story type • recognizes story mood	2 elements present	1 element present	0 elements present	____ x 3 = ____ points
Plot • retells story in correct order • recognizes difference between major events and supporting details	2 elements present	1 element present	0 elements present	____ x 3 = ____ points
Conflict • knows main character's problem • knows why main character has problem	2 elements present	1 element present	0 elements present	____ x 4 = ____ points
Theme • knows what author wants to say • explains theme in 1–3 words	2 elements present	1 element present	0 elements present	____ x 4 = ____ points

28–30 = A
26–27 = B
24–25 = C
21–23 = D
<21 = F

Total score ____ /28 = ____

Plot

■ retells story in correct order

■ recognizes difference between major events and supporting details

Students should be able to recognize the difference between a story-defining event and a detail that supports but does not shape the story and theme. Conduct the following activity with students in small groups or individually. After students read the story, provide them with cards listing several events that took place during the story. Instruct students to arrange the cards in the order the events occurred in the story. Next, have the students separate the ordered pile into major events and supporting details.

Conflict

■ knows main character's problem

■ knows why main character has this problem

After students complete the reading, use a small-group discussion to determine the main character's problem. Before the group members begin their discussion, have each student in the group write down who or what prevents a main character from attaining a certain goal. After the groups have a chance to discuss this topic, have them present a summary of their discussion to the class and discuss the results as a class. Once the class identifies the main character's problem, have students write why the character is having trouble with this situation. Once again, give students a chance to share and elaborate on responses.

Theme

■ knows what author wants to say

■ explains theme in one to three words

During a postreading discussion, ask students what they learned about the character while reading the story. Stimulate discussion by asking questions, such as how did the character change or how did the character remain the same? By exploring character growth, you can guide students toward a discussion of theme, or the author's underlying message to readers. Offer beginning readers a choice of four themes and ask them to vote on which theme they think the story wants to convey. Once the class identifies the correct theme, have students write in their journals a one- to three-word restatement of the theme along with an explanation for why they chose those words.

How to Use the

FICTION Rubric

at the Intermediate Level

Introduce the Rubric

Distribute and briefly discuss the rubric with students before they read the novel or short story. Explain that you will base the assessment on students' recognition of story classification, their ability to recount the story with emphasis on significant details, and their understanding of story conflict and theme. Ask students to keep these areas in mind as they read the novel or short story.

Once students complete the reading, discuss the rubric elements thoroughly, making sure students understand your expectations and know that to receive full credit they must meet the objectives listed.

Make the Assignment

Preview the book with students, discussing any cover illustrations or graphics and the book's title. This brief group exercise gets students ready to read by helping them focus on their purpose for reading. After the discussion, instruct students to read the book silently or, in the case of less mature or emerging readers, allow students to read with a reading buddy.

Assess Student Understanding

Classification
- identifies story type
- recognizes story mood (happy, sad)
- makes comparisons with similar stories

Students at this level should be able to identify the type of story, such as a historical novel or a science fiction story. If students are unsure, instruct them to reflect on those elements that separate the types of stories. For example, historical fiction is always set in the author's past, whereas science fiction and fantasy involve unexplained phenomena and frequently take place in a time period or place not governed by the rules of our time period or planet. Folktales are short, simple stories that have a very explicit message, such as he who hesitates is lost or haste makes waste. Have students defend, verbally or in writing, their choice of story type by listing three reasons for their choice.

READING   # FICTION   INTERMEDIATE

Task: Student will read and respond to a work of fiction.

Goal/Standard: Demonstrate understanding through oral or written response

Criteria	4	3	2	1	Total Points
Classification • identifies story type • recognizes story mood • makes comparisons with similar stories	3 complete elements present	2 complete elements present	1 complete element present	Evidence of 2+ incomplete elements	____ x 3 = ____ points
Plot • retells in correct order • distinguishes major events from supporting details • recognizes subplots	3 complete elements present	2 complete elements present	1 complete element present	Evidence of 2+ incomplete elements	____ x 3 = ____ points
Conflict • identifies main character's struggle • understands why main character is struggling • identifies type of conflict	3 complete elements present	2 complete elements present	1 complete element present	Evidence of 2+ incomplete elements	____ x 4 = ____ points
Theme • knows what author wants to say • restates theme in 1–3 words • identifies passage that conveys story theme	3 complete elements present	2 complete elements present	1 complete element present	Evidence of 2+ incomplete elements	____ x 5 = ____ points

56–60 = A
52–55 = B   Total score ____/60 = ____
47–51 = C
42–46 = D
<42 = F

When students tell why the story is a happy or sad tale, they should be able to provide information from the story as their rationale. For example, a story that contains the tragic death of a major character is sad because of that death. When students offer their choice and reasons for making that choice, instruct them to extend their response by comparing this story with another one that is very similar or very different.

Plot

- retells story in correct order
- distinguishes major events from supporting details
- recognizes subplots

Students should be able to recognize the difference between a story-defining event and a detail that supports but does not shape the story and theme. Instruct students, working in pairs, to use index cards to write several scenes from the story, one scene per card. Next, have students exchange cards and arrange their partner's cards in the proper story sequence. Then have students remove those cards that list minor scenes—that is, scenes that have no direct influence on the story outcome—and respond in writing or verbally why they chose to remove certain cards and leave others.

Conflict

- identifies main character's struggle
- understands why main character is struggling
- identifies type of conflict

The first element in this category asks students to name the specific struggle (Harry Potter vs. Lord Voldemort), and the third element asks students to identify the conflict category (man vs. man). After students read the story, instruct them to write a brief entry in their journals identifying the main character's struggle, including why they think the situation is such a struggle for that character. Next, working in a small or large group, discuss the types of conflict that exist in literature. The types are man versus man, man versus society, man versus self, and man versus nature. Instruct students to reflect on the type of conflict in the story they have just read and, in their journals, identify the conflict along with their reason for choosing it. Correct responses should cite specific information from the story to support a certain choice.

Theme

- knows what the author wants to say
- restates theme in one to three words
- identifies passage that conveys story theme

After students finish reading the story, have them write what they learned while reading the story. Instruct them to reflect on knowledge they gained beyond concrete facts, such as specific information about the main character's job or place of residence, and what they learned by reading the story that will help them in their own lives. Next, instruct students to rewrite what the author was trying to say in one to three words. The word limit helps students focus on what they are trying to say by reducing a message to its simplest terms. On the third card, instruct students to write the passage in the story that represents or makes the author's message clear to readers, citing page and paragraph number.

READING NONFICTION

During the early years of formal education, most reading material is fiction. By the intermediate level, however, students spend approximately half their time exploring nonfiction materials. The use of unfamiliar text structures (description, sequence or process, comparison, cause and effect, and problem and solution, argument, or persuasion) as well as the introduction of charts and graphs and specialized vocabulary present new challenges even for mature readers. Learning to identify text structures is the first step in making predictions about the type of information a specific passage may contain. Activities designed to familiarize students with these structures and a review of how to use context clues to define new vocabulary are worthwhile exercises that increase reader comprehension of a wide variety of nonfiction materials such as the following:

- magazines
- newspapers
- textbooks
- trade books
- reference materials (encyclopedia, dictionary, atlas)
- Web site pages

For a refresher on text structures, visit Web sites for K–12 teachers, such as Teachers.Net (http://www.teachers.net/) and Teachnet.com (http://www.teachnet.com/).

How to Use the
NONFICTION Rubric
at the Primary Level

Introduce the Rubric

Distribute and briefly discuss the rubric with students before they read the nonfiction text. Explain that you will base the assessment on students' understanding of the purpose of the text, their ability to recognize nonfiction format elements, their use of text cues to aid their understanding, and their overall comprehension of text content. Ask students to keep these areas in mind as they read the text.

Once students complete the reading, discuss the rubric elements thoroughly, making sure students understand your expectations and know that to receive full credit they must meet the objectives listed.

Make the Assignment

Before beginning a nonfiction reading assignment, it is a good idea to administer an informal assessment of students' prior knowledge. To accomplish this task quickly, use a graphic organizer, such as a web. Place the topic in the center of the chalkboard or transparency sheet and ask students to provide words or brief phrases that they have heard in association with the topic. Then organize the words and phrases into groups based on their relationship to one another. For example, if the nonfiction article or book deals with the solar system, the students may provide names of planets. Next, group the planet names under the heading "Names of Planets." Repeat this process for all categories of words and phrases until you have organized all of them under headings in the web. Then instruct students to read the selection silently or, in the case of less mature readers, read the selection aloud to them, instructing them to think about additional words or phrases that they could place under each heading.

Assess Student Understanding

Purpose
- identifies topic
- understands author's purpose

The initial identification of the topic will, most likely, take place during the prereading phase. After students complete the reading, instruct them to write three sentences about what they learned from the text. Have reluctant writers tell or draw their responses. Discuss the author's purpose for writing about this topic—was it to teach them those things they learned?

NONFICTION

Task: Student will read and respond to a nonfiction book.

Goal/Standard: Demonstrate understanding through verbal, visual, or written response

Criteria	2	1	0	Total Points
Purpose • Identifies topic • Understands author's purpose	2 elements present	1 element present	0 elements present	____ × 3 = ____ points
Format • Identifies text structure • Understands graphic organizers that display data	2 elements present	1 element present	0 elements present	____ × 3 = ____ points
Content • Uses context clues to learn specialized vocabulary • Understands link between pictures and text	2 elements present	1 element present	0 elements present	____ × 4 = ____ points

19–20 = A
18 = B
16–17 = C
14–15 = D
<14 = F

Total score ____/20 = ____

Format

- identifies text structure
- understands graphic organizers that display data

Before students begin reading nonfiction material, discuss the various arrangements of nonfiction texts. The most basic types are description, sequence (sometimes called process), comparison, cause and effect, and problem and solution (sometimes called persuasion or argument). To help students deal with nonfiction material, display in the classroom graphic organizers for each nonfiction text organization. For the description graphic organizer, use a web with the topic in the center and attributes written on branches extending from the center. For sequence, use a numbered row because order is essential in this type of text. For the comparison organizer, use a Venn diagram to accommodate similarities and differences. For cause and effect, show one line for the effect and several lines extending below it on which to list the causes. For the problem and solution organizer, show two blocks, one listing the problem, the other, a solution. Have examples of the graphic organizers on hand in the classroom and ask students to draw the appropriate organizer for the nonfiction information they have read. Work with students at this level to fill in the organizer with details from the text.

Content

- uses context clues to learn specialized vocabulary
- understands link between pictures and text

After students complete the reading assignment, distribute a worksheet that contains some sentences from the passage or post the sentences on a sheet of tag board. Highlight unfamiliar vocabulary words and ask students to supply, in writing, their definition for each word, explaining why they think theirs is the correct definition. To determine if students understand the link between pictures and text, instruct them to list three things they learned from the text that also appear in the text illustrations.

How to Use the
NONFICTION Rubric
at the Intermediate Level

Introduce the Rubric

Distribute and briefly discuss the rubric with students before they read the nonfiction text. Explain that you will base the assessment on students' understanding of the purpose of the text, their ability to recognize nonfiction format elements, their use of text cues to aid their understanding, and their comprehension of text content. Ask students to keep these areas in mind as they read the text.

Once students complete the reading, discuss the rubric elements thoroughly, making sure students understand your expectations and know that to receive full credit they must meet the objectives listed.

Make the Assignment

Before making a nonfiction reading assignment, it is a good idea to assess students' prior knowledge. Accomplish this task with an oral brainstorming activity or an informal inventory that contains terms associated with the topic and asks students to rate their depth of understanding of the terms on a scale of 1 to 3, with 3 being the highest level of understanding. This activity is helpful at the beginning of a subject area text chapter, such as a science unit on human anatomy or a social studies chapter on government. The inventory may help determine the level of material students can handle for this particular topic.

After determining the degree of prior knowledge, instruct students to read the selection independently and use their reading log to record any questions or observations they have about the material as they read.

Assess Student Understanding

Purpose
- identifies topic
- understands author's purpose
- recognizes significance of topic

READING   **NONFICTION**   INTERMEDIATE

Task: Student will read and respond to a nonfiction book.

Goal/Standard: Demonstrate understanding through verbal, visual, or written response

Criteria	4	3	2	1	Total Points
Purpose • identifies topic • understands author's purpose • recognizes significance of topic	3 complete elements present	2 complete elements present	1 complete element present	Evidence of 2+ incomplete elements	____ x 3 = ____ points
Format • identifies text structure • understands graphic organizers that display data • can convert information on charts and graphs to paragraph form	3 complete elements present	2 complete elements present	1 complete element present	Evidence of 2+ incomplete elements	____ x 3 = ____ points
Content • uses context clues to learn specialized vocabulary • understands link between pictures and text • can compare text information with prior knowledge of topic	3 complete elements present	2 complete elements present	1 complete element present	Evidence of 2+ incomplete elements	____ x 4 = ____ points

37–40 = A
35–36 = B   Total score ____/40 = ____
31–34 = C
28–30 = D
<28 = F

Students will have had the opportunity to identify the topic during the prereading activity. After students complete the reading assignment, discuss the author's purpose for writing about this topic. Instruct them to use their journals to record five things they learned from the reading and how those things will help them in their daily lives.

Format
- identifies text structure
- understands graphic organizers that display data
- can convert information on charts and graphs to paragraph form

---

Briefly review the five basic text organization structures with students, instructing them to create the appropriate organizer for their reading assignment. Then tell them to fill in the organizer with information from the reading passage. Finally, select one chart, graph, or other type of organizer and instruct students to transcribe the organizer's information into paragraph form. For a variation of this assignment, have students state verbally the information in their own words.

Content
- uses context clues to learn specialized vocabulary
- understands link between pictures and text
- can compare text information with prior knowledge of topic

Students at this level are capable of demonstrating their ability to use context clues to learn specialized vocabulary. After students finish the reading assignment, provide them with a list of five to nine unfamiliar vocabulary terms from the text. Instruct them to write the terms and their own definitions for the words. Later, working in small groups, have students compare their definitions with the actual definition from a dictionary. If student responses are incorrect, ask which clues led them to develop their definition. Next, place students in small groups and assign each group an illustration from the passage. Have each group present a comprehensive description of their illustration to the rest of the class by using information from the text to clarify the significance of the picture in relation to the text. For a variation of this activity, have students offer the same explanation in writing in their journals. Finally, instruct students to list five things they knew about the topic before reading the passage. After they have read the assignment, instruct them to write beside each item any new information they received that confirmed or contradicted their prior knowledge. Ask students to verbally clarify unclear or incorrect responses.

READING BIOGRAPHY

Although fiction is populated by imaginary characters who live, play, work, and even die at an author's whim, biographies recount the exploits of real people.

Authors of fiction are free to manipulate characters or other literary elements such as conflict and setting to convey their message. Biographers must decide whether a subject's life bears retelling, then extract the theme from actual events that took place in that subject's life.

The benefit of reading biographies lies in the subject's connection to the reader, such as a shared background (single parent household, only child) or interest (sports, music). When readers perceive this connection, they develop an immediate empathy for the subject and gain insight into dealing with similar obstacles that arise in their own lives.

Several varieties of biographies are available to readers. The following list describes the most popular types:

- Authentic biography is a well-documented and carefully researched account of a person's life. Its construction follows many of the same rules as serious works written for adults. Examples include Jean Fritz's *And Then What Happened, Paul Revere?* and Russell Freedman's *The Wright Brothers: How They Invented the Airplane.*

- Partial biographies chronicle only part of the subject's life (a liberty extended to children's authors), usually focusing on a point of high drama in the subject's life. Examples include Alice Fleming's *George Washington Wasn't Always Old.*

- Fictionalized biography is grounded in research but lets the author dramatize certain events and personalize the subject, rather than present the type of straight reporting found in authentic biography. Examples include F. N. Monjo's *Letters to Horseface: Young Mozart's Travels in Italy* and Jean Fritz's *Homesick: My Own Story,* a fictionalized autobiography about the author's early childhood in China.

- Biographical fiction consists entirely of imagined conversations and constructed events. Examples of this form include Robert Lawson's *Ben and Me,* about a mouse who lived in Ben Franklin's old fur cap, and Robert Lawson's *Mr. Revere and I,* told from the point of view of Paul Revere's horse, Scheherazade.

How to Use the
BIOGRAPHY Rubric
at the Primary Level

Introduce the Rubric

Distribute and briefly discuss the rubric with students before they read the biography. Explain that you will base the assessment on students' recognition of the author's purpose for writing the biography, their ability to discern the format of the text, and their understanding of the value and accuracy of the text. Ask students to keep these elements in mind as they read the biography.

Once students complete the reading, discuss the rubric elements thoroughly, making sure students understand your expectations and know that to receive full credit they must meet the objectives listed.

Make the Assignment

Briefly review the definition of biography (an account of the life of a real person) with students, discussing why the lives of some people are worth a creating record for others to read. Then instruct students to read the story silently or, in the case of less mature readers, read the story aloud to the class.

Assess Student Understanding

Purpose
- knows significance of subject
- understands subject's role in shaping history

After students complete the reading, instruct them to write a letter to the biographical subject thanking the person for the role he or she played in shaping history. Display the letters on a classroom bulletin board. When assessing the letters, look for reference to specific accomplishments in the subject's life that had a dramatic influence on the past, present, and future.

READING   # BIOGRAPHY   PRIMARY

Task: Student will read and respond to a biography.

Goal/Standard: Demonstrate understanding through verbal, visual, or written response

Criteria	2	1	0	Total Points
Purpose • knows significance of subject • understands subject's role in shaping history	2 elements present	1 element present	0 elements present	____ × 3 = ____ points
Format • distinguishes between biography and historical fiction • distinguishes between complete and partial biography	2 elements present	1 element present	0 elements present	____ × 3 = ____ points
Content • identifies subject's accomplishments • can compare account with nonfiction for accuracy	2 elements present	1 element present	0 elements present	____ × 4 = ____ points

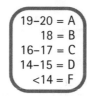

19–20 = A
18 = B
16–17 = C
14–15 = D
<14 = F

Total score ____/20 = ____

Format
- distinguishes between biography and historical fiction
- distinguishes between complete and partial biography

After students complete the reading, conduct a discussion about the difference between biography (authentic) and historical fiction (loosely based on historical facts or events). Then ask students to vote secretly (only you will see students' names on the paper ballots) on whether the account was biography or historical fiction. Next, discuss complete and partial biographies and ask students to vote secretly on whether the account was a complete or partial biography. Have students include a reason for their choice.

Content
- identifies subject's accomplishments
- can compare account with nonfiction for accuracy

After students complete the reading, instruct them to compile a list of the subject's accomplishments. Then provide encyclopedia and Internet access to verify if other sources credit the subject with the same or different accomplishments.

How to Use the
BIOGRAPHY Rubric
at the Intermediate Level

Introduce the Rubric

Distribute and briefly discuss the rubric with students before they read the biography. Explain that you will base the assessment on students' recognition of the author's purpose for writing the biography, their ability to discern the format of the text, and their understanding of the value and accuracy of the text. Ask students to keep these elements in mind as they read the biography.

Once the reading is complete, discuss the rubric elements, making sure students understand your expectations and know that to receive full credit they must meet the objectives listed.

Make the Assignment

Discuss the term *biography* with students first, asking them why they believe this individual's life is worthy of retelling. Then instruct students to read the account independently or with a reading buddy.

Assess Student Understanding

Purpose
- knows significance of subject
- understands subject's role in shaping history
- recognizes subject's influence on past, present, and future

After students complete the reading, instruct them to act as journalists and write an account of at least one of the subject's accomplishments, including in their article how this achievement affected the past, present, and future. Display the completed articles.

READING   **BIOGRAPHY**   INTERMEDIATE

Task: Student will read and respond to a biography.

Goal/Standard: Demonstrate understanding through verbal, visual, or written response

Criteria	4	3	2	1	Total Points
Purpose • knows significance of subject • understands subject's role in shaping history • recognizes subject's influence on past, present, and future	3 complete elements present	2 complete elements present	1 complete element present	Evidence of 2+ incomplete elements	____ x 3 = ____ points
Format • distinguishes between biography and historical fiction • distinguishes between complete and partial biography • identifies point of view of storyteller	3 complete elements present	2 complete elements present	1 complete element present	Evidence of 2+ incomplete elements	____ x 3 = ____ points
Content • identifies subject's accomplishments • can compare account with nonfiction for accuracy • links subject's deeds to readers' lives	3 complete elements present	2 complete elements present	1 complete element present	Evidence of 2+ incomplete elements	____ x 4 = ____ points

37–40 = A
35–36 = B   Total score ____/40 = ____
31–34 = C
28–30 = D
<28 = F

Format
- distinguishes between biography and historical fiction
- distinguishes between complete and partial biography
- identifies point of view of storyteller

After students complete the reading, instruct them to vote (secretly on paper ballots containing their names) on whether the work is biography or historical fiction. Tell them to include the reason for their choice. On a second secret ballot, instruct students to identify the work as a complete or partial biography and why they made that choice. Finally, ask students to assume the identity of the author and write in their journals why they wanted to tell the story of the biographical subject.

Content
- identifies subject's accomplishments
- can compare account with nonfiction for accuracy
- links subject's deeds to readers' lives

After students complete the reading, instruct them to compile a list of the subject's accomplishments. Next, have students use a second source (encyclopedia, Internet) to verify the information found in the account. Finally, have students write in their journals the ways the biographical subject's actions have affected their lives or the lives of others in this time period.

COMPREHENSION MONITORING

The National Reading Panel found that comprehension monitoring is an effective strategy for enhancing students' ability to understand what they have read (National Institute of Child Health and Human Development, 2000). This approach, which is an extrapolation of the behaviors found in mature and effective readers, helps students develop awareness of when they are not understanding a selection and then implement fix-up strategies to increase their comprehension. This situation occurs more frequently in expository text with its vocabulary challenges and varied text formats. Teachers can introduce comprehension monitoring by modeling it for the class while reading a passage containing unfamiliar terms or format. As readers approach challenging new texts, they can be taught to notice how these texts are different from more familiar texts. Teachers also model fix-up strategies for reading these challenging texts. Students are encouraged to go backward or forward in the text to find those words and phrases with which they are familiar, using these items as a foundation for dissecting the meaning of the new text. After demonstrating this think-aloud method for students, teachers can facilitate the experience by working with readers in smaller groups.

How to Use the Comprehension
MONITORING Rubric
at the Intermediate Level

Introduce the Rubric

Discuss and distribute the rubric prior to making the assignment. Explain that you will base the assessment on students' awareness of their own comprehension levels, their ability to recognize unfamiliar text, and their ability to select and implement fix-up strategies. Remind students that to receive full credit they must achieve the stated criteria.

Make the Assignment

Placing students in pairs, triads, or small groups, assign a reading selection from one of their content subjects, such as science or social studies. As readers progress through the text, have them check with one another about their understanding of the text. As a new word or phrase appears in the text, instruct readers to stop, indicate which word or phrase is not familiar, and then look back and forward in the passage to determine the meaning of the unfamiliar section. To practice this skill, students could be asked to write their observations as well as their guesses about the passage meaning in informal journals that could be discussed during the postreading phase of the lesson.

Assess Student Understanding

Awareness
- distinguishes between familiar and unfamiliar text
- dissects meaning of phrases

Mature readers have a clear sense of what they know and what they don't know, making it less difficult for them to deal with the appearance of new material within a reading passage. Less experienced readers tend to dissect meaning a word at a time, losing the opportunity to see how the words relate to one another and give meaning to an entire phrase or passage.

Recognition
- identifies unfamiliar text
- explains why the text is unfamiliar

MONITORING

Task: Students, working in pairs or triads, will be able to practice comprehension monitoring strategies.

Goal/Standard: Students will meet stated criteria.

Criteria	2	1	0	Total Points
Awareness • distinguishes between familiar and unfamiliar text • dissects meaning of phrases	2 complete elements present	1 complete element present	0 complete elements present	_____ × 3 = _____ points
Recognition • identifies unfamiliar text • explains why the text is not familiar	2 complete elements present	1 complete element present	0 complete elements present	_____ × 3 = _____ points
Response • selects strategy to determine meaning • implements strategy effectively	2 complete elements present	1 complete element present	0 complete elements present	_____ × 3 = _____ points

17–18 = A
15–16 = B
14 = C
13 = D
<13 = F

Total score _____/18 = _____

At the heart of comprehension monitoring is the ability to recognize that not all words and phrases are familiar to even the most experienced reader. Those words and phrases must be dealt with by using strategies designed to help determine meaning. Less mature readers can be taught to better recognize unfamiliar and challenging words and text formats.

Response
- selects strategy to determine meaning
- implements strategy effectively

After realizing that a reading passage contains unfamiliar text or format, readers must (through self-training that involves practice and repetition) identify an effective strategy for determining meaning and moving forward in the passage. The two most common strategies are moving backward and forward in the text to see where this unfamiliar section fits in the big picture. For example, if a reader encounters an in-depth description of a type of bird in the midst of a passage about African wildlife, it might be a good idea to backtrack to see which types of creatures were being discussed just before this section. Likewise, if readers have difficulty following a sequential passage about how a tornado is formed, it may prove helpful to move forward in the text to the actual emergence of the tornado to see where specific steps fit into the equation. Teaching students these strategies and providing them with opportunities for practice will develop more confident and mature readers.

Rubrics for Fictional Story Elements

4

> Peggy, the school librarian, is working with teachers on a project to help students make more informed literature choices. By determining students' understanding of literary elements, Peggy hopes to find clues to their method of selecting books. Mature readers rely on certain factors such as genre, specific character types, or story settings to choose new books to read, whereas inexperienced readers rely on more superficial elements, such as book length or cover illustration. Peggy decides to design rubrics that measure student understanding of literary elements.

KNOW THE READ AHEAD

Rather than selecting the same book repeatedly, mature readers are able to identify those elements they enjoyed in a book to initiate a search for similar material. For example, if readers know that they like to read stories set in another time period, past or future, they can use that preference to make other selections in historical or science fiction. Readers who gravitate to plots containing suspense or mystery can turn to books of that genre for a guaranteed satisfying read. Less experienced readers, however, may become frustrated in their search for new reading materials because they are unable to identify those elements that they find enjoyable in previous books and must depend on less reliable elements, such as cover illustrations, for choosing new books.

Readers who possess a clear understanding of literary elements become lifelong readers because they know how to select materials they are likely to enjoy. Executing and assessing activities that focus on understanding plot, characterization, setting, point of view, and theme help students develop literature selection skills that will serve them beyond classroom walls.

Some of these elements, such as plot, also appear in Chapter 3; however, that chapter focuses on overall comprehension of a text, whereas this chapter, with its focus on individual literary elements, gives teachers a chance to test the depth of student understanding of story structure. In addition, Chapter 3 covers several types of reading material, whereas this chapter focuses on fictional literature.

PLOT

Use one or two of the activities described in this section to help students think about the plot, or sequence of events, in a story. Some are discussion options, and others require a written or artistic response, but all encourage students to start thinking in terms of sequence, struggle or conflict, summary, and prediction and prepare them for the assessment activity. The activities focus on students' ability to recount sequence, recognize major events (vs. supporting details), and demonstrate understanding of the struggle or conflict in the story. Students can complete most of the activities individually, in pairs, or in small groups; however, some activities, such as the Directed Reading-Thinking Activity, are effective with an entire classroom of students. Appropriate grade levels follow the activity description: P = primary, I = intermediate. Base the assessment on student participation in these preliminary workshops, the discussions stemming from them, and the suggested assessment activities that correspond with the rubrics.

- Construct a timeline of major events that take place during the story and use different-colored markers to denote their level of importance in the story's outcome. I

- Write a newspaper article (include who, what, where, when, how, and why) about what happens in the story. Newspaper space is limited, so make certain students include only the most important information. I

- Participate in a Directed Reading-Thinking Activity (Stauffer, 1969) in a large or small group, making predictions about what will happen next in the story. P/I (for primary students, teachers read the story aloud in a Directed Listening-Thinking Activity)

- Construct a class or small-group mural depicting the major and minor events of a story and arranging the pictures in sequential order. P/I

- Select a favorite story and tell it to classmates, focusing on the order in which events occur. P/I

- Draw a series of pictures that depict the sequence of a story. P/I

How to Use the
PLOT Rubric
at the Primary Level

Introduce the Rubric

Distribute and briefly discuss the rubric with students before they read the story. Explain that you will base the assessment on their understanding of sequence and their ability to recognize story conflict, predict upcoming events in the story, and summarize the story. Ask students to keep these elements in mind as they read.

After reading the story, discuss the rubric elements thoroughly, making sure students understand your expectations and know that to receive full credit they must meet the objectives listed.

Make the Assignment

Discuss the story title and cover illustration (if available) before you begin reading so that students can think about the type of story they will read. Read the story aloud to students or, in the case of more mature readers, allow them to follow along with their own copies of the book or short story or to read silently.

Assess Student Understanding

Prediction
- predicts next event in sequence
- uses prior knowledge to make predictions

Conduct this activity before you finish reading the story aloud or before students finish the story if they are reading independently. Instruct students to work individually (through writing) or in groups (verbally) to make educated guesses about what they think will happen next in the story. Move among students and, when necessary, prompt them with open-ended questions (What do you think will happen?) and ask them to explain their prediction (Why do you feel that way?). Note which students are consistently able (or unable) to make accurate predictions. In the students' reasons for their predictions, consider how they use information from the earlier part of the story. For example, if students hear or read that two of the three Billy Goats Gruff go over the bridge, they should be able to predict the third crossing. An inappropriate answer and its accompanying reason would contain no information from the earlier part of the story.

READING   **PLOT**   PRIMARY

Task: Student will participate in activities that focus on story plot.

Goal/Standard: Demonstrate understanding of plot through verbal or written response

Criteria	2	1	0	Total Points
Prediction • predicts next event in sequence • uses prior knowledge to make predictions	2 elements present	1 element present	0 elements present	____ x 4 = ____ points
Sequence • has no substitutions or omissions in oral retelling • has no reversal of events in oral retelling	2 elements present	1 element present	0 elements present	____ x 3 = ____ points
Conflict (struggle) • identifies characters' struggle • describes type of struggle	2 elements present	1 element present	0 elements present	____ x 4 = ____ points
Summary • summarizes major events • excludes minor details	2 elements present	1 element present	0 elements present	____ x 4 = ____ points

28–30 = A
26–27 = B
24–25 = C   Total score ____ /30 = ____
21–23 = D
<21 = F

Sequence
- has no substitutions or omissions in oral retelling
- has no reversal of events in oral retelling

Begin by placing students in small groups, instructing them to discuss the events in the story with one another. If you haven't already, introduce the term *brainstorming* and demonstrate how to brainstorm about events in the story. Provide students with index cards in two different colors and have them write major events—ones that had a direct and dramatic effect on the main character or story outcome—on one color of card (one event per card) and supporting details (one detail per card) on the other color of cards. Challenge students to place the event cards in the proper sequence—first with their own cards, then with a classmate's event cards.

Conflict (Struggle)
- identifies characters' struggle
- describes type of struggle

Discuss the meaning of conflict or struggle, using grade-level appropriate language to share the four main types of story conflict—man versus man, man versus self, man versus nature, man versus society. Provide literary examples of each type of struggle. Ask students to identify which type of conflict or struggle exists in the story and explain their choice.

Summary
- summarizes major events
- excludes minor details

Assign a word count of no more than 50 to 75 words and have students write a summary of the story. Or, for a verbal version of this assignment, assign a time limit (no more than 5 minutes) in which students must recount the entire story. To prevent students from simply repeating what their classmates say, it is a good idea to complete the oral option during reading conferences when you meet individually with students to discuss what they are reading. You might also conduct the oral option with a group of students or even the whole class, with each student providing one event in the plot sequence. Another alternative is to assign a time limit and allow two or more students to dramatize the entire story. With a limit on the amount of time or number of words students can use, they must make decisions about eliminating less significant events and details from their retelling.

How to Use the

PLOT Rubric

at the Intermediate Level

Introduce the Rubric

Distribute and briefly discuss the rubric with students before they read the story. Explain that you will base the assessment on their understanding of sequence, ability to recognize story conflict, ability to predict upcoming events in the story, and, after completing their reading, ability to summarize the story. Ask students to keep these elements in mind as they read the story.

Once they complete the reading, discuss the rubric elements thoroughly, making sure students understand your expectations and know that to receive full credit they must meet the objectives listed.

Make the Assignment

Initiate a brief discussion based on the story title about the type of story the students will read. This exercise helps students focus on their purpose for reading. After the discussion, instruct students to read the story silently.

Assess Student Understanding

Prediction
- predicts next event in sequence
- uses prior knowledge to make predictions
- predicts story climax

Conduct this activity while students are still reading the story. Assign a section or chapter. Then instruct students to work individually (through writing) or in groups (verbally) to make educated guesses about what they think will happen next in the story. Move among students and, when necessary, prompt them with open-ended questions (What do you think will happen?) and ask them to explain their prediction (Why do you feel that way?). Note which students are consistently able (or unable) to make accurate predictions. An appropriate response has evidence that the student reflected on the story to make his or her predictions. For example, a student might respond, "I feel this way because the last time something like this happened to the main character she reacted this way, so I figured she would react that way again."

READING **PLOT** INTERMEDIATE

Task: Student will participate in activities that focus on plot.

Goal/Standard: Demonstrate understanding through verbal or written response

Giving 0 points can be an option—no evidence, no credit.

Criteria	4	3	2	1	Total Points
Prediction • predicts next event in sequence • uses prior knowledge to make predictions	3 complete elements present	2 complete elements present	1 complete element present	Evidence of 2+ incomplete elements	____ x 5 = ____ points
Sequence • has no substitutions or omissions in oral retelling • has no reversal of events in oral retelling	3 complete elements present	2 complete elements present	1 complete element present	Evidence of 2+ incomplete elements	____ x 3 = ____ points
Conflict (struggle) • identifies characters' struggle • describes type of struggle • can compare with struggles in other stories	3 complete elements present	2 complete elements present	1 complete element present	Evidence of 2+ incomplete elements	____ x 3 = ____ points
Summary • summarizes major events • excludes minor details • understands why certain details are not vital to story outcome	3 complete elements present	2 complete elements present	1 complete element present	Evidence of 2+ incomplete elements	____ x 4 = ____ points

56–60 = A
52–55 = B   Total score ____ /60 = ____
47–51 = C
42–46 = D
<42 = F

Sequence

- has no substitutions or omissions in oral retelling
- has no reversal of events in oral retelling
- emphasizes major events in oral retelling

Have students brainstorm individually or in small groups about events in the story. Distribute in two different colors index cards and have students write major events—ones that had a direct and dramatic effect on the main character or story outcome—on one color of card (one event per card) and supporting details (one detail per card) on the other color of card. Challenge students to place the event cards in the proper sequence—first, with their own cards, then with a classmate's cards. Collect the cards to see whether students have listed major events and supporting details correctly on the colored cards.

Conflict (Struggle)

- identifies characters' struggle
- describes type of struggle
- can compare with struggles in other stories

Discuss the meaning of conflict, sharing the four main types of story conflict or struggle—man versus man, man versus self, man versus nature, man versus society—and providing literary examples of each type of conflict or struggle. Have students offer literary examples of the different types of struggle as well. Ask them to identify which type of struggle exists in the story they read and to explain their choice. Have students compare the struggles in the literary examples they provided to determine which story struggles are similar and which are not.

Summary

- summarizes major events
- excludes minor details
- understands why some details are not vital to story outcome

Students might fulfill this objective through one of three methods. Assign a word count (no more than 100 to 125 words) and have students write a summary of the story. For a verbal version of this assignment, assign a time limit (no more than 5 minutes) in which the student must recount the entire story. (Use student conference time for verbal responses, working with individual students while others are involved in exercises that do not require direct instruction.) A third alternative is to assign a time limit and allow two or more students to dramatize the entire story. With a limit on the amount of time or words students can use, they must make decisions about eliminating less significant events and details from their retelling.

CHARACTER

Readers tend to be drawn to or repelled from a story based on the connection they have with the characters, so it is a good idea for readers to spend time getting to know these individuals during and after the reading of the story. Authors use characters to convey a story's theme, or underlying message, and if readers do not connect with the characters, they miss the author's message.

The activities in this section require students to focus on the main character(s) in the story. Some activities ask students to provide information from the story, such as creating a Venn diagram to compare characters with each other or the reader, whereas other activities ask students to extrapolate new information based on what they have read. For example, drawing a character's bedroom requires the student to reflect on what is important to that character (sports, music, friends) and include it in the drawing. Also, the character's personality (shy, outgoing, creative) would influence the decor (paint color, technique, theme of wallpaper border) and the overall appearance (neat, cluttered, cozy) of the room.

Getting Underway

Conduct some workshop activities to get students thinking about characterization in fiction. Some suggestions for activities appear in this section. Appropriate grade levels follow the activity description: P = primary, I = intermediate. Base the assessment on student participation in these preliminary workshops and the discussions stemming from these and the suggested assessment activities that correspond with the rubric. The first few times students complete this type of assignment, allow them to work in pairs or triads, thus fostering discussion about characters. As students become more comfortable with the assignment, they can work independently.

- Draw or describe a character's bedroom. Include the belongings there that bring the character happiness as well as the color and style of the furnishings. P/I

- Create a character "zoo," drawing and describing which animal each of the characters might be and how the characters would behave with one another. P/I

- Write letters to one of the story characters, offering advice or encouragement regarding the character's planned course of action. I

- Plan and celebrate a birthday party for the story's main character. Use the color scheme, decorations, food, and games that the character would enjoy most. Draw or construct a gift for the character. P/I

- Use videotape, still camera, or drawing supplies to create a day in the life of the story's main character, recounting with pictures what that character does during the course of a normal day. I

How to Use the
CHARACTER Rubric
at the Primary Level

Introduce the Rubric

Distribute the rubric to students, discussing it briefly before they read the story. Explain that the assessment will focus on students' ability to describe the character and compare that character with other characters as well as with themselves. They are also expected to draw inferences about the character based on the character's words and actions and to evaluate the character's behavior. Remind students to keep these tasks in mind as they read the story.

After reading the story, discuss the rubric elements thoroughly, making sure students understand your expectations of them and know that to receive full credit they must meet the objectives listed.

Make the Assignment

Read the story aloud to students or, in the case of more mature readers, instruct students to follow along with their own copies of the story or to read silently.

Assess Student Understanding

Description
- describes character appearance
- describes character personality

For this objective, devise activities that require students to describe physical, mental, and emotional aspects of the story character(s). Make sure students can give reasons for their responses based on the text. For example, you might give the following instructions:

- Physical—pretend you are the main character. Look in the mirror. Describe what you see.

- Mental—pretend you are the main character. Write a letter to a friend telling him or her how school is going this year. What are your favorite subjects? Which ones give you the most trouble? Use information the author provides about the character to determine which subjects would be easy or difficult for the character. Does the author describe the character as organized, poetic, or artistic?

READING # CHARACTER PRIMARY

Task: Student will participate in activities that focus on characterization.

Goal/Standard: Demonstrate understanding through verbal, visual, or written response

Criteria	4	3	2	1	Total Points
Description • describes character appearance • describes character personality	2 elements present	1 element present	1+ incomplete elements	0 elements present	____ x 3 = ____ points
Comparison • compares characters based on physical description • compares characters based on actions	2 elements present	1 element present	1+ incomplete elements	0 elements present	____ x 3 = ____ points
Inference • links behavior to personality traits • predicts behavior based on personality traits	2 elements present	1 element present	1+ incomplete elements	0 elements present	____ x 4 = ____ points
Evaluation • identifies behaviors in specific situations as wise or foolish • identifies character as good or evil	2 elements present	1 element present	1+ incomplete elements	0 elements present	____ x 5 = ____ points

28–30 = A
26–27 = B   Total score ____ /60 = ____
24–25 = C
21–23 = D
<21 = F

• Emotional—pretend you are the main character and write one or two entries in your diary explaining how you feel before, during, or after an event [teacher supplies event]. Use what you have learned from the story about the character and how he or she behaves and reacts to imagine what that character might feel.

Comparison
■ compares characters based on physical description
■ compares characters based on actions

Comparison activities have two related components. First, students must demonstrate ability to identify a character's attributes (physical, mental, emotional) and then compare these attributes with those of another character or with their own attributes. Students should give accurate descriptions of character traits and specific locations in the text where characters exhibit these attributes.

Inference
■ links behavior to personality traits
■ predicts behavior based on personality traits

The ability to determine what a story character might think or say requires readers to use information in the book to form their response. A written or dramatized response to inferential questions requires readers to make inferences based on information the story provides and what they already know—their prior knowledge—about human nature. For example, consider the following question: What career would the story character choose and why? If readers think a lively, outgoing boy would be happy as a monk, they may have ignored or misread the story cues that indicate the boy would be happier and more fulfilled in a job that involves more interaction with people. Be sure students offer an explanation for why they think the character would be a good doctor, teacher, or dictator, for example.

Evaluation
■ identifies behaviors in specific situations as wise or foolish
■ identifies character as good or evil

Once readers are able to infer, or predict, character responses to a certain situation, they can use this information to evaluate the character's behavior. If, for example, a character's stubbornness, illustrated by the character's refusal to make even the smallest compromise, causes the character to lose a friend, readers might judge this behavior as negative. Instruct students to write letters to characters, sharing their opinion of the character's behavior along with advice about how to alter a negative situation—for example, "Try listening to other people's ideas" or "Be willing to make some compromises." If a student fails to see the role a character's stubbornness plays in the breakup of a friendship, ask how the student would feel if he or she were the character's friend.

How to Use the
CHARACTER Rubric
at the Intermediate Level

Introduce the Rubric

Distribute the rubric to students, discussing it briefly before they read the story. Explain that the assessment will focus on their ability to describe the character and compare that character with other characters as well as with themselves. They are also expected to draw inferences about the character based on the character's words and actions and to evaluate the character's behavior. Remind students to keep these tasks in mind as they read the story.

Once they complete the reading, discuss the rubric elements thoroughly, making sure students understand your expectations and know that to receive full credit they must meet the objectives listed.

Make the Assignment

Instruct students to read the story silently.

Assess Student Understanding

Description
- describes character appearance
- describes character personality
- links character actions to personal tastes

Devise activities that require students to describe physical, mental, or emotional aspects of the story character(s). Make sure students can give reasons for their responses based on the text. For example, you might give the following instructions:

- Physical—pretend you are the main character. Look in the mirror. Describe what you see.

- Mental—pretend you are the main character. Write a letter to a friend telling him or her about how school is going this year. What are your favorite subjects? Which ones give you the most trouble? Use information the author provides about the character to determine which subjects would be easy or difficult for the character. Does the author describe the character as organized, poetic, or artistic?

READING   # CHARACTER   INTERMEDIATE

Task: Student will participate in activities that focus on characterization.

Goal/Standard: Demonstrate understanding through verbal, visual, or written response

Criteria	4	3	2	1	Total Points
Description • describes character appearance • describes character personality • links character actions to personal tastes	3 complete elements present	2 complete elements present	1 complete element present	Evidence of 2+ incomplete elements	_____ x 3 = _____ points
Comparison • compares characters based on physical description • compares characters based on actions • compares character's behavior with that of real people	3 complete elements present	2 complete elements present	1 complete element present	Evidence of 2+ incomplete elements	_____ x 3 = _____ points
Inference • links behavior to personality traits • predicts behavior based on personality traits • predicts how character's behavior will affect story outcome	3 complete elements present	2 complete elements present	1 complete element present	Evidence of 2+ incomplete elements	_____ x 4 = _____ points
Evaluation • identifies behavior in specific situations as wise or foolish • identifies character as good or evil • understands character's actions	3 complete elements present	2 complete elements present	1 complete element present	Evidence of 2+ incomplete elements	_____ x 5 = _____ points

56–60 = A
52–55 = B
47–51 = C
42–46 = D
<42 = F

Total score _____ /60 = _____

- Emotional—pretend you are the main character and write one or two entries in your diary explaining how you feel before, during, or after an event [teacher supplies the event]. Use what you have learned from the story about the character to imagine what that character might feel.

Comparison

- compares characters based on physical description
- compares characters based on actions
- compares character's behavior with that of real people

Comparison activities have two related components. Students must be able, first, to identify the character's characteristics and, second, to contrast these attributes with the attributes of another character or with their own attributes. Readers should pay attention to the physical, mental, and emotional attributes an author ascribes to a character, including those such as courage, honesty, and humor. For physical characteristics, students should look beyond height, weight, and color of hair to such details as neat or scruffy appearance. Also under physical characteristics are character's actions. Mentally, a slow-witted or naive person might not make the same kinds of judgments as a very bright person. Emotionally, characters' thoughts tell a lot about how they will react to situations. Activities that ask the student to respond to comparison questions require students to make this type of comparison. Consider the following question: Why would (or wouldn't) you want to have the story character as a best friend? Students might, for example, want to have the character Harry Potter as a friend because they admire and aspire to emulate some of his attributes, such as bravery and honesty. Students' responses may be verbal or written. Look for students' ability to describe character traits accurately and locate places in the text where characters exhibit these attributes.

Inference

- links behavior to personality traits
- predicts behavior based on personality traits
- predicts how character's behavior will affect story outcome

The ability to determine what a story character might think or say requires readers to use information in the book to form their response. A written or dramatized response to inferential questions requires readers to make inferences based on information the story provides and what they know—their prior knowledge—about human nature. Consider the following question: What career would the story character choose and why? If readers think a lively, outgoing boy would be happy as a monk, they may have ignored or misread the story cues that indicate the boy would be happier and more fulfilled in a job that involves more interaction with people. Be sure students offer some explanation for why they think the character would be a good doctor, teacher, or dictator, for example.

Evaluation

■ identifies behaviors in specific situations as wise or foolish
■ identifies character as good or evil
■ understands character's actions

Once readers are able to infer, or predict, character responses to a certain situation, they can use this information to evaluate that character's behavior. If, for example, a character's stubborn attitude, illustrated in the story by the character's refusal to make even the smallest compromise, causes the story character to lose a friend, readers might judge this behavior as negative. Instruct students to write letters to story characters, sharing their opinion of the character's behavior along with advice about how to alter a negative situation—for example, "Try listening to other people's ideas" or "Be willing to make some compromises." If a student fails to see the role a character's stubborn attitude plays in the breakup of a friendship, ask how the student would feel if he or she were the character's friend.

SETTING

Before evaluating students on their understanding of the role setting plays in fiction, try some of these workshop activities to get students thinking about describing, comparing, and contrasting various story settings before proceeding to the rubric activities. Activities that focus on story setting help students gain an increased awareness of the influence time and place have on the story outcome. Activities that require students to describe, compare, and contrast various story settings provide the basis for later, more in-depth study of why certain times and places are more critical to a story's plot and outcome.

Appropriate grade levels follow the activity description: P = primary, I = intermediate. Base the assessment on student participation in these preliminary workshops and the discussions stemming from these and the suggested assessment activities that correspond with the rubric. The first few times students complete this type of assignment, allow them to work in pairs or triads, thus fostering discussion about setting. As students become more comfortable with the assignment, they can work independently.

- Draw a series of various settings in the story, arranging them in the order of their importance to the story outcome. P/I

- Construct a Venn diagram comparing two or more of the story settings. I

- Create a diorama of one of the story's main settings, making sure to include items that are significant to the plot or character. P/I

- Pretend to be a tour guide and conduct a guided tour of the story's main settings, pointing out important features to "tourists." P/I

- Write a poem about the story settings. Include verses for each important setting and a refrain to unite the composition. P/I

- Construct a Venn diagram comparing the story setting with your own environment. I

How to Use the
SETTING Rubric
at the Primary Level

Introduce the Rubric

Distribute and briefly review the rubric before reading the book or story. Explain to students that the assessment will focus on their understanding of the importance of setting on character behavior and story outcome and that they will examine various settings to determine which are most and least important to these areas.

After students read the book or story, discuss the rubric elements thoroughly, making certain students understand your expectations and know that to receive full credit they must meet the objectives listed.

Make the Assignment

Read the story aloud or, in the case of more mature readers, instruct students to follow along with their own copies of the story or to read silently.

Assess Student Understanding

Description
- provides sensory account of setting
- understands attributes of primary setting (time period, time of day, climate)

The more information readers gather and internalize regarding story setting, the easier it is for them to decide the influence setting has on a character's response, behavior, and choices. For example, if a story character is afraid of thunderstorms and is stranded alone during a particularly violent outburst, that character may do or say things that are somewhat out of character. If students fail to see any connection between the story character and this setting, initiate a discussion about how students feel when it is dark, sunny, bitterly cold, windy, and so on to point out the influence weather can have on an individual. You might have students respond orally to the following questions:

- How do you think the story character will behave during a thunderstorm and why?

- Think about something that frightens you. How do you behave during this situation?

- Are you more or less likely to help another person? To behave calmly? To feel the way you usually feel?

READING   # SETTING   PRIMARY

Task: Student will participate in activities that focus on setting.

Goal/Standard: Demonstrate understanding through verbal, visual, or written response

Criteria	2	1	0	Total Points
Description • provides sensory account of setting • understands attributes of primary setting	2 elements present	1 element present	0 elements present	_____ x 3 = _____ points
Comparison • sees differences between settings • compares setting with real life	2 elements present	1 element present	0 elements present	_____ x 3 = _____ points
Inference • understands importance of setting • explains influence of setting on story	2 elements present	1 element present	0 elements present	_____ x 4 = _____ points
Evaluation • identifies setting as safe or unstable location • explains character's response to setting	2 elements present	1 element present	0 elements present	_____ x 5 = _____ points

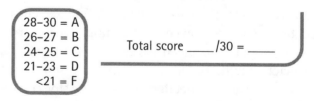

28–30 = A
26–27 = B
24–25 = C
21–23 = D
<21 = F

Total score _____ /30 = _____

For the assessed activity, have students use all five senses to create a "picture" of the primary story setting. Acceptable responses should identify the story's main setting correctly and give a complete (five senses) sensory recreation of that setting. Students can complete this activity in writing or verbally during student reading conference time.

Comparison
■ sees differences between settings
■ compares setting with real life

The ability to compare settings within a single story or between those in the story and those in real life helps students see the influence story setting can have on character behavior and, ultimately, story outcome. Finding scenes where characters face similar problems in different settings is one way of determining the extent of the role setting plays in the characters' actions. Have students use a Venn diagram to illustrate the similarities and differences between different settings within the story and between the story setting and real life. Members of a reading group can share their completed Venn diagrams verbally. For another activity, have students choose a scene where two characters face the same problem; then, in writing or in a dramatization in pairs, have students describe how each of the characters behaves. Or, using two stories, have students choose a similar scene and tell, in writing or in a dramatization in pairs, how the characters in each story handle the situation. To ensure no two dramatizations are the same for these last two options, write scenes on strips of paper and have pairs of students draw the slips of paper randomly. Discuss the reasons students believe the characters respond the way they do.

Inference
■ understands importance of setting
■ explains influence of setting on story

The ability to infer, or make predictions about, how a character will respond in a particular setting is another way of examining the role story setting plays in story outcome. A painfully shy character, for example, thrust into a very public situation might behave differently than he or she would in a situation that allowed the person to remain anonymous. The highly visible setting might cause the shy character to come out of his or her shell and reach out to others, thus altering the story outcome.

Compile a list of several settings and probable character responses (fear, calmness, happiness). Before students complete the reading, provide them with the settings and character responses and ask them to match the setting with the character's probable response. After matching the setting and response, have students write a brief statement (two to four sentences) about why they think the character would react in that way.

Evaluation
- identifies setting as safe or unstable location
- explains character's response to setting

Have students give an artistic response for this activity. Instruct them to draw the story character in a setting where the character would be most at home, such as a cowboy on a ranch, a teacher in a classroom, or a child on a playground. Ask them to draw a second picture depicting the character in the most uncomfortable setting, such as a small child wandering through a dense and dark forest. A brief discussion with each student could clarify any doubts about the quality of the response.

How to Use the

SETTING Rubric

at the Intermediate Level

Introduce the Rubric

Distribute and briefly review the rubric before reading the novel or short story. Explain to students that the assessment will focus on their understanding of the importance of setting on character behavior and story outcome and that they will examine various settings to determine which are most and least important to these areas.

After students read the book or story, discuss the rubric elements thoroughly, making certain students understand your expectations and know that to receive full credit they must meet the objectives listed.

Make the Assignment

Instruct students to read the story with their reading buddies or alone silently.

Assess Student Understanding

Description
■ provides sensory account of setting
■ understands attributes of primary setting (time period, time of day, climate)
■ sketches primary setting

The more information readers gather and internalize regarding story setting, the easier it is for them to decide the influence setting has on a character's response, behavior, and choices. For example, if a story character is afraid of thunderstorms and is stranded alone during a particularly violent outburst, that character may do or say things that are somewhat out of character. If students fail to see any connection between the story character and this setting, initiate a discussion about how those students feel when it is dark, sunny, bitterly cold, windy, and so on to point out the effect weather can have on an individual. Have students write a journal entry and respond to these questions:

- How do you think the story character will behave during the thunderstorm? Why?

- Think about something that frightens you. How do you behave during this situation?

READING   **SETTING**   INTERMEDIATE

Task: Student will participate in activities that focus on setting.

Goal/Standard: Demonstrate understanding through verbal, visual, or written response

Criteria	4	3	2	1	Total Points
Description • provides sensory account of setting • understands attributes of primary setting • sketches primary setting	3 complete elements present	2 complete elements present	1 complete element present	Evidence of 2+ incomplete elements	____ x 3 = ____ points
Comparison • sees differences between settings • compares setting with real life • lists similarities and differences between two settings	3 complete elements present	2 complete elements present	1 complete element present	Evidence of 2+ incomplete elements	____ x 3 = ____ points
Inference • understands importance of setting • explains influence of setting on story • identifies setting elements that influence outcome	3 complete elements present	2 complete elements present	1 complete element present	Evidence of 2+ incomplete elements	____ x 4 = ____ points
Evaluation • identifies setting as safe or unstable location • explains character's response to setting • identifies importance of setting on story outcome	3 complete elements present	2 complete elements present	1 complete element present	Evidence of 2+ incomplete elements	____ x 5 = ____ points

56–60 = A
52–55 = B   Total score ____ /60 = ____
47–51 = C
42–46 = D
<42 = F

- Are you more or less likely to help another person? To behave calmly? To feel the way you usually feel?

Then have students sketch the setting and use colors to signify those areas that have greater influence on the story. Have students create a word "picture" of the primary story setting to accompany the sketch. Acceptable responses should identify the story's main setting correctly and give a complete (five senses) sensory recreation of that setting.

Comparison

- sees differences between settings
- compares setting with real life
- lists similarities and differences between two settings

The ability to compare settings within a single story or between the story and real life helps students see the influence story setting can have on character behavior and, ultimately, story outcome. Finding scenes where characters face similar problems in different settings is one way of determining the extent of the role setting plays in the characters' actions. Have students use a Venn diagram to illustrate the similarities and differences between different settings within the story and between the story setting and real life. Members of a reading group can share their completed Venn diagrams verbally. For another activity, have students choose a scene where two characters face the same problem; then, in writing or in a dramatization in pairs, students can tell how each of the characters behaves. Or, using two stories, have students choose a similar scene and tell, in writing or in a dramatization in pairs, how the characters in each story handle the situation. To ensure no two dramatizations are the same, write scenes on strips of paper and have pairs of students randomly draw the slips of paper. Discuss the reasons students believe the characters respond the way they do.

Inference

- understands importance of setting
- explains influence of setting on story
- identifies setting elements that influence outcome

The ability to infer, or make predictions about, how a character will respond in a particular setting is another way of examining the role story setting plays in story outcome. A painfully shy character, for example, thrust into a very public situation might behave differently than he or she would in a situation that allowed the person to remain anonymous. The highly visible setting might cause the shy character to come out of his or her shell and reach out to others, thus altering the story outcome. Before students complete the reading, provide them with several settings and several character responses and ask them to match up the setting with the character's probable response.

Evaluation
- identifies setting as safe or unstable location
- explains character's response to setting
- identifies importance of setting on story outcome

Readers can evaluate story settings from a number of perspectives. They might examine setting from the viewpoint of the main character and examine that character's behavior, stating whether the behavior is wise or foolish in different settings. Readers might also identify the various story settings as safe and secure or unstable for the story characters. Another method of evaluating story setting is to make judgments on whether the author chose a good backdrop to tell the story. In a story set in Victorian England, for example, it would be difficult to portray a female character as completely free to do as she wishes given the constraints of society during that period. For the assessment activity, have students write a journal entry analyzing the influence of the setting on the story outcome. To support their opinions about setting influence, tell students to describe a different setting for the story and explain how placing the story in that setting would change the story outcome.

THEME

When students read fiction, they tend to think more in terms of plot and characterization than story theme. The theme, or author's underlying message, is the thread that runs through the entire story, binding plot, characters, and setting. To prepare students for a more formal evaluation of their understanding of story theme, conduct some of the suggested workshop activities that follow while they read the assigned text. These activities help students think about how the author uses character interaction in various situations to convey a specific message. The activities encourage students to focus on identifying the author's underlying message and the author's effectiveness in conveying that message to readers.

Appropriate grade levels follow the activity description: P = primary, I = intermediate. Base the assessment on student participation in these preliminary workshops and the suggested assessment activities that correspond with the rubric. The first few times students complete this type of assignment, allow them to work in pairs or triads, thus fostering discussion about theme. As students become more comfortable with the assignment, they can work independently.

- Write a letter to remind yourself of ways to apply the story's theme to your own daily life. P/I

- Find real-life examples of the story's theme in the daily newspaper, such as a real-life example of "love one another" or "good triumphs over evil," common literature themes. I

- Select scenes from the story that illustrate the theme and work in small groups to act out those scenes for classmates. P/I

- Find and share a natural object (leaf, stone) or a picture of an element of nature (storm, tree) that embodies the story theme and explain why the element of nature reminds you of the theme. I

- Design and draw a symbol that represents the story's theme and explain why you chose certain elements to create the symbol, such as clasped hands if the theme is "reaching out to others" or a symbol that incorporates a sunrise if the theme is "each day brings new promise." I

- Reflect on the story's theme and brainstorm alone or in a small group about sensory images (sight, sound, taste, touch, smell) that remind you of the theme as in the examples that follow: sight, a sunrise for the theme of "new beginnings"; sound, triumphant brass section to symbolize "good over evil"; taste and smell, homemade bread with a theme of "there's no place like home"; and touch, the feel of a warm hand wrapped around your own hand for a theme of "I'll always be there for you." P/I

How to Use the

THEME Rubric

at the Primary Level

Introduce the Rubric

Distribute and briefly review the rubric before reading the story. Explain to students that the assessment will focus on their understanding of the author's underlying message and how the author uses plot, characters, and setting to convey that idea. Ask students to keep these ideas in mind as they read.

After students read the book or story, discuss the rubric elements thoroughly, making certain students understand your expectations and know that to receive full credit they must meet the objectives listed.

Make the Assignment

Read the story aloud or, in the case of more mature readers, have the students follow along in their own copies of the story or read it silently.

Assess Student Understanding

Identification
- knows author's message
- knows story event that contains author's message

Use verbal, written, or artistic activities to determine students' ability to identify the author's message. For example, have students give the story a new title that conveys the theme. Then, have them create a book poster, placing the new title across the top of the poster. Below the title, have them draw the scene that conveys the main theme. At the bottom of the poster, instruct students to write a sentence or two paraphrasing the author's message. Students' inability to complete any or all of these tasks may indicate that they have only a literal understanding of plot.

READING   **THEME**   PRIMARY

Task: Student will participate in activities that focus on theme.

Goal/Standard: Demonstrate understanding through verbal, visual, or written response

Criteria	2	1	0	Total Points
Identification • knows author's message • knows story event that contains author's message	2 elements present	1 element present	0 elements present	_____ x 3 = _____ points
Comparison • identifies stories with similar theme • links appropriate character with theme	2 elements present	1 element present	0 elements present	_____ x 3 = _____ points
Application • finds real-life examples of theme • draws or locates pictures emphasizing theme	2 elements present	1 element present	0 elements present	_____ x 4 = _____ points
Evaluation • expresses feelings regarding the story theme • determines whether other stories with the same theme convey theme more or less effectively	2 elements present	1 element present	0 elements present	_____ x 5 = _____ points

28–30 = A
26–27 = B
24–25 = C
21–23 = D
<21 = F

Total score _____ /30 = _____

Comparison

■ identifies stories with similar themes
■ links appropriate character with theme

Comparing stories with similar themes but different plots requires students to examine the stories for common elements that convey the underlying message. As a class, create a list of stories with similar themes but different plots. Then, have students select one and explain in one or two sentences how the story is similar to the assigned story. Next, ask students to compare story characters in the assigned story to determine which character—not always the main character—most effectively conveys the author's message. Have students create a three-way Venn diagram, with two circles representing two characters and a third circle representing ideas (honesty, bravery) related to the theme. Ask students to identify which character conveys the theme more accurately by demonstrating the elements more often.

Application

■ finds real-life examples of theme
■ draws or locates pictures emphasizing theme

An author's primary purpose for incorporating a theme in a story is to give readers something to think about that will, perhaps, change their lives in a positive way. Once students are able to identify the story's theme, instruct them to connect that message in some way with their own lives. For example, if the story's theme is to treat others as you would like to be treated, initiate a discussion that helps students reflect on their behavior and how closely that behavior measures up to the story theme. Have students create a collage of pictures that emphasize the theme and share the reasons for their choices in a small-group sharing exercise.

Evaluation

■ expresses feelings regarding the story theme (agrees/disagrees with underlying message)
■ determines whether other stories with the same theme convey theme more or less effectively

Even young readers should be able to identify the story theme and offer their opinion about it. After identifying the story theme, have students write their feelings regarding that theme. In their response, have students identify other stories with the same theme that they consider more or less effective in conveying the theme. As an alternative assignment, have students record their responses for you to listen to.

How to Use the

THEME Rubric

at the Intermediate level

Introduce the Rubric

Distribute and briefly review the rubric before reading the novel or short story. Explain to students that the assessment will focus on their understanding of the author's underlying message and how the author uses plot, characters, and setting to convey that idea. Ask students to keep these ideas in mind as they read the novel or short story.

After students read the book or story, discuss the rubric elements thoroughly, making certain students understand your expectations and know that to receive full credit they must meet the objectives listed.

Make the Assignment

Instruct students to read the story with their reading buddies or alone silently.

Assess Student Understanding

Identification
- knows author's message
- knows story event that contains author's message
- restates author's message in a single statement

To determine students' ability to identify the author's message, ask them to give the story a new title that conveys the theme. Then have them describe the scene or event that conveys the theme and write the author's message in one sentence. Students' inability to complete these tasks may indicate that they have only a literal understanding of plot.

Comparison
- identifies stories with same themes
- links appropriate character with theme
- compares stories with similar theme for similarities and differences in plot development

Comparing stories with similar themes but different plots requires students to examine the stories for common elements that convey the underlying

READING   # THEME   INTERMEDIATE

Task: Student will participate in activities that focus on theme.

Goal/Standard: Demonstrate understanding through verbal, visual, or written response

Criteria	4	3	2	1	Total Points
Identification • knows author's message • knows story event that contains author's message • restates author's message in a single statement	3 complete elements present	2 complete elements present	1 complete element present	Evidence of 2+ incomplete elements	____ x 3 = ____ points
Comparison • identifies stories with similar themes • links appropriate character with theme • compares stories with same theme for similarities and differences in plot development	3 complete elements present	2 complete elements present	1 complete element present	Evidence of 2+ incomplete elements	____ x 3 = ____ points
Application • finds real-life examples of theme • draws or locates pictures emphasizing theme· • explains how theme applies to reader's life	3 complete elements present	2 complete elements present	1 complete element present	Evidence of 2+ incomplete elements	____ x 4 = ____ points
Evaluation • rates theme by personal opinion • determines whether other stories with same theme convey theme more or less effectively • judges author's success in conveying theme	3 complete elements present	2 complete elements present	1 complete element present	Evidence of 2+ incomplete elements	____ x 5 = ____ points

56–60 = A
52–55 = B
47–51 = C
42–46 = D
<42 = F

Total score ____ /60 = ____

message. Ask students to name two stories with similar themes. Have them create a Venn diagram that illustrates the way the two stories are alike and different in plot development. By comparing such facets as how the story introduces conflict and the use of subplots to support the theme, students can discern a pattern in the development of similar-themed stories. For example, stories whose theme is "love conquers all" typically contain an event that takes the lovers apart, but their desire to be together drives them toward reunion, as in the drama *Romeo and Juliet*. Next, have students compare story characters in the assigned story to determine which character most effectively conveys the author's message. Have students create a three-way Venn diagram with two circles representing two characters and a third circle representing ideas (honesty, bravery) related to the theme. Ask students to identify which character conveys the theme best by demonstrating the elements more often.

Application

- finds real-life examples of theme
- draws or locates pictures emphasizing theme
- explains how theme applies to reader's life

An author's primary purpose for incorporating a theme in a story is to give readers something to think about that will, perhaps, change their lives in a positive way. Once readers are able to identify the story's theme, instruct them to connect that message in some way with their own lives. For example, if the story's theme is "treat others as you would like to be treated," initiate a discussion that helps students reflect on their behavior and how closely that behavior measures up to the story theme.

Evaluation

- rates theme by personal opinion
- determines whether other stories with the same theme convey theme more or less effectively
- judges author's success in conveying theme

In addition to identifying the story theme, more mature readers should be able to find its meaning in their own lives and determine whether the author did an effective job of conveying the theme. Discuss with students whether they find the theme carefully woven into story events and characters' responses to a variety of situations or whether the theme is didactic and explicit, deliberately drawing the readers' attention with phrases like "and the moral of this story is . . ." or "what this story has taught us is . . ." Ask students to choose a scene that best conveys the theme and write, in their own words, a journal entry that explains why they believe that scene conveys the theme. Tell them also to state whether they agree with the story's theme.

Rubrics for Assessing Student Writing

5

Concerns over student writing scores on state proficiency tests have prompted school leaders in the Midland district to examine their current instructional methods. At a meeting to discuss solutions, Janet, a primary-level teacher and member of the district's literacy committee, suggests adopting a rubric assessment method. In addition to providing students with guidelines for completing written assignments, rubrics pinpoint individual weaknesses, streamlining remedial sessions. Chuck, an intermediate-level teacher, adds that teachers can modify rubrics for specific writing assignments. The meeting chair asks Janet and Chuck to present the rubrics assessment approach to the entire faculty.

RUBRICS ENHANCE INSTRUCTION

Janet and Chuck are not alone in their belief that assessment with rubrics can actually enhance the instructional phase of writing. The rubric acts as a blueprint for instruction, highlighting which criteria teachers should introduce and reinforce with students; therefore, for the rubric to be most effective, teachers must construct and share it with students before students begin the writing assignment.

THE FIVE-STEP WRITING PROCESS

Rubric assessment allows teachers and students to focus on a writing assignment as a process rather than as an isolated product. And rather than assessing just the product (a specific type of writing, such as a research paper, description, letter, etc.), teachers assess each step in the widely accepted five-step writing process—prewriting, drafting, revising, editing, and publishing. Teachers can gain valuable insight concerning student writing performance with a rubric assessment of the five-step process because the process requires certain behaviors and skills at each step. In addition, teachers at all levels can use a single rubric for the five-step writing process because the process does not change.

GETTING UNDER WAY

A prewriting activity should precede the actual drafting process in all writing exercises. During the prewriting stage, students discuss with their peers and their teacher their topic and their audience—what they want to write and whom they want to read it. This activity provides student authors with an opportunity to focus on a topic and make decisions about how to organize the material for the audience. Making these decisions early in the writing process makes subsequent steps less difficult. The following items are examples of writing stimuli for all children at all grade levels:

- Field trip or guest speaker

- Film or video

- Work of literature

- Group discussion of a specific topic (rainforests, friendship, conflict)

- Participation in a simulation (mayor for a day, mock city government meetings)

The prewriting stage should follow as soon as possible after students have completed one of these activities, or any activity that stimulates thinking and imagination. The more time that passes between the experience and the prewriting activity, the less likely students will recall information that could enhance their compositions. Student authors can complete prewriting activities as a class, in small groups, or individually.

How to Use the

FIVE-STEP WRITING PROCESS Rubric

at the Primary and Intermediate Levels

Introduce the Rubric

Young authors need to understand that composing is just one part of the writing process. Equally important to the creation of a written product are prewriting, revising, editing, and publishing. The sequence and procedure of this five-step writing process remain consistent no matter what the writing assignment.

Before the writing assignment, share the rubric with students, reviewing the steps of the writing process. The format of the assignment directs the decisions young authors must make during the prewriting stage, such as the why (purpose), how (format), and who (audience) of their proposed composition and how they plan to share the writing (publishing), but it is critical that young authors understand the need for the steps that will help them convey their ideas to an audience.

Make the Assignment

The writing assignment can be any type, structure, and length appropriate to the grade level.

Assess Student Understanding

Whether writing instruction takes place in a workshop or lecture format, the criteria students must meet during the steps of the writing process do not change, and students must participate in each step to demonstrate understanding of the writing process.

Prewriting
- identifies topic and purpose
- identifies form
- identifies audience
- uses graphic organizers to relate ideas

Students must identify topic, purpose, form, and the intended audience for their composition before they begin writing. Meet briefly with each student early in the writing process to determine the topic the student has chosen. After students select a topic, student-teacher or small-group discussion can guide students toward the most effective way to organize their composition. By answering two questions—Why am I writing about this topic? What do I want to tell readers about this topic?—students should be able, with minimal guidance, to select a suitable format for their ideas. For example, students who wish to share their thoughts about current conditions in the regional or global environment with an elected official will decide quickly that the most effective form for such communication is a formal letter. Primary students may find a paragraph is the best format for telling the rest of the class about their favorite summer vacation.

Decisions about form also stem from the intended audience for the composition. In the case of the letter on the environmental topic, the intended audience might be one or more elected officials. Because of these individuals' knowledge of the situation, students can assume some prior knowledge and use more advanced environment-related terminology in their letter. Students writing about their favorite vacation destination should include a description for those classmates who may not be familiar with the location. To assess student understanding at the prewriting step, have students share in a written or verbal format what they are writing about, why they chose the topic, what they hope to convey, and whom they would like to read their ideas. Provide students with concrete examples and keep samples available for examination in the classroom. You can also work with students in small or large groups to discuss which formats work best for various purposes.

Drafting

- generates and organizes ideas
- composes lead statement
- develops appropriate topic sentence
- writes rough draft

Students may first wish to organize their ideas by using an outline or graphic organizer such as a web to ensure that they include important points and details. After composing the critical lead statement designed to arouse audience interest, students can complete an initial draft of the composition, getting their thoughts on paper. They can give attention to spelling and grammatical errors in later steps. To help students work on good lead statements, have them read their opening statements aloud to one another to see if the statement gets readers interested in reading more. Like a good newspaper lead statement, the student author's lead statement should draw readers in and make them want more information. Allow students a significant number of drafting sessions during class time so you can monitor student work habits. Keep the time frame for writing fairly brief to ensure that students are not trying to correct and rewrite at this phase. For teachers, this is the most hands-off part of the writing process because writing is a solitary exercise.

WRITING **FIVE-STEP WRITING PROCESS** PRIMARY AND INTERMEDIATE

Task: Student will produce a written composition by using the five-step writing process.

Goal/Standard: Demonstrate understanding of the writing process through written sample

Criteria	4	3	2	1	Total Points
Prewriting • identifies topic and purpose • identifies form • identifies audience • uses graphic organizers to relate ideas	4 complete elements present	3 complete elements present	2 complete elements present	1 complete element present	____ x 4 = ____ points
Drafting • generates and organizes ideas • composes lead statement • develops appropriate topic sentence· • writes rough draft	4 complete elements present	3 complete elements present	2 complete elements present	1 complete element present	____ x 4 = ____ points
Revising • rereads rough draft • shares with partner(s) • makes changes based on feedback • creates unifying title	4 complete elements present	3 complete elements present	2 complete elements present	1 complete element present	____ x 4 = ____ points
Editing • proofreads for errors • creates edit checklist • makes corrections • shares edited draft with partner(s)	4 complete elements present	3 complete elements present	2 complete elements present	1 complete element present	____ x 4 = ____ points
Publishing • adds illustrations or graphics • identifies appropriate method for sharing work • incorporates media when appropriate • shares with intended audience	4 complete elements present	3 complete elements present	2 complete elements present	1 complete element present	____ x 4 = ____ points

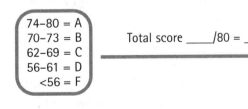

74–80 = A
70–73 = B
62–69 = C
56–61 = D
<56 = F

Total score ____/80 = ____

Revising

- rereads rough draft
- shares with partner(s)
- makes changes based on feedback
- creates unifying title

Assign students to work in pairs or triads to read one another's compositions so student authors can receive feedback not only from the teacher but also from classmates. Make sure students read the work aloud to one another; the verbal recitation helps them hear poor or awkward phrasing. Before working in revision groups, provide students with guidelines for feedback exercises. For example, you might tell students they must offer one positive comment for each criticism. Also, student critics must give specific examples of what they like and dislike about the work rather than a generic statement such as "I like what you wrote." The more specific information helps student authors make corrections. You might also share a piece of student writing in need of work with the entire class and have students revise it as a group, offering ideas for ways to improve the content, organization, style, and so on. You gain information about student understanding when you hear their ideas, and the student author receives many options for revising the piece.

Editing

- proofreads for errors
- creates edit checklist
- makes corrections
- shares edited draft with partner(s)

You and your students can conduct the more objective exercise of editing by using a checklist of criteria to check for errors and make corrections before submission of the final draft. The checklist should list such areas as spelling, punctuation, capitalization, and grammar and include places for classmates, the student author, and the teacher to initial that they have checked the composition before students return to their revision groups for a final read of the material. You might create a checklist with two columns: One column is for peer editors to check off, indicating that they have checked spelling, grammar, and so on, and the other column is for you. Check the work after the peer editors and return it to the student author to make any corrections. Base the grade for the editing element on how well students correct the mistakes, not on the number of initial mistakes.

Publishing

- adds illustrations or graphics
- identifies appropriate method for sharing work
- incorporates media when appropriate
- shares with intended audience

During this final step of the writing process, students can work individually or in small groups or participate in a more general class discussion as they reflect on the inclusion of any illustrations, photos, graphics, or media that might enhance their work. Give students time to gather feedback from classmates. For media, students might use music in the background of a poetry reading or use a slide show to accompany a nonfiction article. Primary students can use a CD or cassette player, while intermediate-level students might use a slide show or PowerPoint presentation. Next, work with each student to reach a consensus about how to share the work. In the example of the letter to the elected official about the environment, the final step would involve addressing an envelope and mailing the letter to its intended audience. Students might share other writing in a different way; for example, a student poet might read his or her poem from the author's chair. Newsletters, author's chair, and anthologies are only a few ways to accomplish the publishing element. Assessment at this step is a last look at the polished product, which should be error-free and accomplish whatever purpose (entertainment, information) was set forth in the prewriting phase.

SIX-TRAIT WRITING

Whereas the five-step writing process provides students with a start-to-finish method for preparing, refining, and sharing their written compositions, the six-trait writing approach has emerged as a comprehensive tool for turning reluctant writers into fluent, enthusiastic authors. The system, developed in the late 1980s in Oregon by a team of educators led by Vickie Spandel, enables teachers to pinpoint the strengths and weaknesses of each student writer, making it possible to tailor instruction to highlight only those areas where assistance is needed. A combination of the six traits—ideas, word choice, conventions, voice, sentence fluency, and organization—can be identified in the works of published authors whose stories students can examine prior to their own writing experiences. Assessment rubrics for six-trait writing activities are universal because the six traits remain constant for all grades. The level of expertise required can be determined by individual teachers who can modify existing assessment rubrics for their specific student population.

The presentation of a six-trait writing rubric should occur near the conclusion of class discussion and experimentation with the method. One effective approach to helping students recognize the six traits is to provide examples in popular children's literature that are familiar to most students. During such activities, encourage students to note how such things as an author's word choice can have a dramatic effect on how they feel about a story. More mature readers may note that they like the way a favorite author "speaks" in each of that author's stories (voice). They may also see that certain authors tend to write a good deal about a particular idea, which might suggest that author's interest in the topic.

How to Use the
SIX-TRAIT WRITING Rubric
at the Primary and Intermediate Levels

Introduce the Rubric

Distribute and discuss the rubric with students prior to the writing assignment. Review the terms to determine if students are clear about their definitions. Whereas subsequent rubrics in this chapter deal with specific types of writing, this rubric can be used and modified to fit most writing assignments. It might be advisable to use the six-trait assessment rubric earlier in the year to familiarize students with this approach. Then, throughout the year, return to the rubric to ensure that students are continuing to follow the guidelines for developing a topic for a written account.

Make the Assignment

Instruct students to select a topic for a writing activity. This can be done as part of a science or social studies unit with students selecting smaller topics within a general heading (e.g., writing about what life on Mars might be like during a unit on the solar system). Encourage students to select a topic that interests them because that interest (or lack thereof) should be reflected in their author's voice. If desired, guidelines for length may be provided. Essay length does not need to be required: The emphasis should be on the quality of the composition rather than an arbitrary page or word count. The more practice students acquire in writing, the more comfortable they will become with expressing their thoughts and ideas on paper.

Assess Student Understanding

Ideas
- clearly interested in topic
- displays knowledge of topic
- looks at topic in a fresh way

Word Choice
- uses vivid describers
- uses powerful verbs
- creates lingering images

WRITING **SIX-TRAIT WRITING** PRIMARY AND INTERMEDIATE

Task: Student will use the six-trait writing method to complete a composition.

Goal/Standard: Demonstrate understanding of six-trait writing method through composition

Criteria	4	3	2	1	Total Points
Ideas • clearly interested in topic • displays knowledge of topic • looks at topic in fresh way	3 complete elements present	2 complete elements present	1 complete element present	Evidence of 2+ incomplete elements	____ x 3 = ____ points
Word choice • uses vivid describers • uses powerful verbs • creates lingering images	3 complete elements present	2 complete elements present	1 complete element present	Evidence of 2+ incomplete elements	____ x 3 = ____ points
Conventions • uses correct spelling • uses correct grammar • uses correct punctuation	3 complete elements present	2 complete elements present	1 complete element present	Evidence of 2+ incomplete elements	____ x 3 = ____ points
Voice • enthusiasm about topic • involves reader • consistent tone	3 complete elements present	2 complete elements present	1 complete element present	Evidence of 2+ incomplete elements	____ x 3 = ____ points
Sentence fluency • variety of sentences • smooth flow throughout • balance of ideas/details	3 complete elements present	2 complete elements present	1 complete element present	Evidence of 2+ incomplete elements	____ x 3 = ____ points
Organization • strong beginning • logical body • clear conclusion	3 complete elements present	2 complete elements present	1 complete element present	Evidence of 2+ incomplete elements	____ x 3 = ____ points

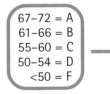

67–72 = A
61–66 = B   Total score ____/72 = ____
55–60 = C
50–54 = D
<50 = F

Convention

■ uses correct spelling

■ uses correct grammar

■ uses correct punctuation

Voice

■ enthusiasm about topic

■ involves reader

■ consistent tone

Sentence Fluency

■ variety of sentences

■ smooth flow throughout

■ balance of ideas/details

Organization

■ strong beginning

■ logical body

■ clear conclusion

This rubric could be used effectively after students have completed a rough draft and made editing changes to correct spelling, grammar, and punctuation. While students are becoming familiar with this type of instruction, it might be a good idea for teachers to highlight those passages that demonstrate evidence of the components listed on the rubric. For example, if a particular sentence shows the author's genuine interest in a topic, teachers might indicate with a note in the margin so that students will be able to replicate this approach in future compositions.

NARRATIVE WRITING—LET ME TELL YOU ABOUT IT

The increased popularity of stories and movies that make use of a narrator to tell the story from an objective point of view makes this format worth investigating in the writing classroom. The storyteller's ability to take a step back from the events and, perhaps, offer some insight into the thoughts and actions of the characters provides readers and writers with a fresh perspective. Differing from earlier narrative writing, mostly found in fairy and folk tales, modern narrative writing maintains its objective viewpoint but brings the readers closer to the characters and their motives while creating a lush and vivid description of the world these characters inhabit. In narrative nonfiction writing, the author takes on the task of introducing readers to a particular topic as though they have had little or no contact with that topic prior to reading the article. To this end, nonfiction narrators must use all five senses to bring topics to life for readers, using a balance of major ideas and details to stimulate reader interest. The rubric in this section can be used as is or with slight modifications for fictional and nonfiction narrative because the primary focus of the assessment is in the narrator's ability to stay focused on the size and vivid description of the topic.

How to Use the
NARRATIVE WRITING Rubric
at the Primary and Intermediate Levels

Introduce the Rubric

Distribute and discuss the rubric with students prior to making the narrative writing assignment. It's a good idea to introduce student authors to journal writing, an informal type of narrative writing, prior to working with more structured assignments. Make sure students understand the narrator's role of introducing readers to the topic by stimulating interest from the onset of the article or story. Challenge student authors to identify ways to actively involve their readers as early as possible. The middle and conclusion of the narrative may be very compelling, but a weak beginning often prompts readers to abandon the article almost immediately.

Make the Assignment

Determine, beforehand, whether to have students write a fiction or nonfiction narrative so that instructional efforts can be focused in a single direction. When choosing fictional narrative, instruct students to tell a brief story (one to two pages for primary; two to four pages for intermediate) taking the role of narrator. In this capacity, it is the student author's responsibility not only to let readers know what is happening in the story but also to provide a vivid mind's-eye view of the story environment. Read some fictional narrative passages from popular children's literature to give students an idea of how narrative writing sounds. For nonfiction, such as the student author's account of something in real life or the introduction of a specific topic, the rules for narrative writing change slightly as student authors attempt to vividly recount an event in their own lives or share information about a specific topic with an audience.

Assess Student Understanding

Topic
- appropriate for narrative format
- appropriate scope/size
- relevant to author and audience

Mechanics
- correct spelling
- correct grammar
- correct punctuation

WRITING **NARRATIVE WRITING** PRIMARY AND INTERMEDIATE

Task: Students will write (fiction/nonfiction) using the narrative form.

Goal/Standard: Demonstrate understanding with completion of narrative composition

Criteria	4	3	2	1	Total Points
Topic • appropriate for narrative format • appropriate scope/size • relevant to author and audience	3 complete elements present	2 complete elements present	1 complete element present	Evidence of 2+ incomplete elements	____ x 3 = ____ points
Mechanics • correct spelling • correct grammar • correct punctuation	3 complete elements present	2 complete elements present	1 complete element present	Evidence of 2+ incomplete elements	____ x 3 = ____ points
Format • clear narrative voice • vivid sensory description • balance of major ideas and details	3 complete elements present	2 complete elements present	1 complete element present	Evidence of 2+ incomplete elements	____ x 3 = ____ points

33–36 = A
31–32 = B
28–30 = C
25–29 = D
<25 = F

Total score ____/36 = ____

Format
- clear narrative voice
- vivid sensory description
- balance of major ideas and details

Keep the rubric at hand while evaluating student compositions. Note authors' ability to engage their audience early in the composition and their use of major ideas and supporting details to keep readers interested. Be aware of student authors' ability to speak in a clear narrative voice, especially in fictional narrative, when it may become easier to assume the identity of one of the characters. The overall composition should have an objective viewpoint that informs readers without attempting to sway their opinion in a particular way.

PERSUASIVE WRITING—LET ME "SELL" YOU ABOUT IT

Whereas narrative writing seeks to inform and, in some cases, entertain the reader, persuasive writing emerges from a slightly different perspective: The purpose of a persuasive article is to convince readers to agree with or, at the very least, understand the author's point of view. Commercial advertising is one of the most common forms of persuasive writing as advertisers seek to convince consumers to become their customers. To that end, many commercial ads tell as much or as little of the facts as necessary to have the most dramatic impact on their arguments. The most effective persuasive writing does not rely on such manipulation but simply presents a strong argument for agreeing with the author.

Whereas students in early years of school may not possess the reasoning and logic required to produce an effective persuasive composition, intermediate-level writers can do a basic type of persuasive writing by selecting an issue (reducing pollution) or practice (wearing seat belts) about which they have strong feelings. This enthusiasm will fuel the young authors' desire to convince or persuade readers to see their viewpoint.

Using this approach, rather than a random, less personal topic allows student writers to become more actively engaged in the composing process and will, no doubt, result in more dramatic and incisive articles.

How to Use the

PERSUASIVE WRITING
Rubric
at the Intermediate Level

Introduce the Rubric

Distribute and discuss the rubric at the beginning of the assignment. Make certain that students possess a clear definition of the term *persuasive* and how it applies to their written composition. Remind students that their completed composition must have all the required elements to achieve the highest grade.

Make the Assignment

Because persuasive writing is a relatively new concept to students at this grade and ability level, it is often more productive to begin with a topic in which they are personally invested. Instruct students to select a topic that has personal importance in their lives (caring for animals, creating a cleaner environment) and, during a prewriting session, make a list or web of why this issue means so much to them. Then, for the writing portion of the assignment, have students write a brief article (one to two pages) using an effective beginning to get readers interested before making their case about why readers should share their beliefs about the topic.

Assess Student Understanding

Topic
- appropriate for format
- relevant to writer and audience
- appropriate scope for format

Mechanics
- accurate spelling
- accurate grammar
- accurate punctuation

Format
- convincing arguments offered
- effective use of factual material
- clear distinction between fact and opinion

PERSUASIVE WRITING

Task: Student will produce a piece of persuasive writing.

Goal/Standard: Completed persuasive writing

Criteria	4	3	2	1	Total Points
Topic • appropriate for format • relevant to author and audience • appropriate scope for format	3 complete elements present	2 complete elements present	1 complete element present	Evidence of 2+ incomplete elements	_____ x 3 = _____ points
Mechanics • accurate spelling • accurate grammar • accurate punctuation	3 complete elements present	2 complete elements present	1 complete element present	Evidence of 2+ incomplete elements	_____ x 3 = _____ points
Format • convincing arguments offered • effective use of factual material • clear distinction between fact and opinion	3 complete elements present	2 complete elements present	1 complete element present	Evidence of 2+ incomplete elements	_____ x 3 = _____ points

33–36 = A
31–32 = B
28–30 = C
25–29 = D
<25 = F

Total score _____ /36 = _____

WRITING ASSIGNMENT RUBRICS

These rubrics cover student-authored fiction, greeting cards, autobiographies, informational brochures, and letters. All of the rubrics and suggested activities are based on use of the five-step writing process and, in most cases, can also make use of the six-trait writing method.

The writing assignment rubrics offer teachers a clear example of what is age- and grade-level appropriate for student authors, rather than simply noting the presence or absence of specific skills (the format of the rubrics in Chapters 3 and 4). The rubrics arrange the required elements in columns rather than under a main heading in the first column. This format of listing full-credit responses provides teachers with more concrete examples of what they may see in student work. Because writing is a generative process (as opposed to the more receptive nature of reading), it is a good idea for teachers to have these concrete guidelines for what a certain student response is worth and when a particular response receives full credit. The more specific nature of these rubrics helps teachers easily identify student submissions as above or below normal expectations for that age and grade level.

Fiction: Amazing Authors

These rubrics assess students' use of the five-step writing process to compose a short work of fiction that demonstrates their understanding of the interaction of plot, character, setting, and theme. The goal, or highest degree of accomplishment on the rubric, for each grade level follows:

- Primary—student creates a work with a logical plot sequence, believable characters, a well-described setting, and a clear theme relevant to plot events.

- Intermediate—student creates a work with a plot sequence that balances major and minor events, two or three believable characters who respond predictably to story conflict, and a vivid setting relevant to plot.

Greeting Card: It's in the (Greeting) Cards

These rubrics assess students' use of the five-step writing process to create a greeting card that demonstrates their understanding of an occasion-appropriate greeting. Students have the option of creating a birthday, holiday, thinking-of-you, hello, get well, sympathy, friendship, or goodbye card. The goal, or highest degree of accomplishment on the rubric, for each grade level follows:

- Primary—student creates a greeting card with a two- or three-color cover, an occasion-appropriate message, and no mechanical errors.

- Intermediate—student creates a greeting card with a full-color, illustrated cover design, an occasion-appropriate message, and excellent overall quality.

Autobiography: It's My Life

These rubrics assess students' use of the five-step writing process to compose an autobiography consisting of text and pictures. Students must demonstrate their understanding of appropriate autobiographical content and photos. The goal, or highest degree of accomplishment on the rubric, for each grade level follows:

- Primary—student creates an autobiography with a well-designed cover that includes text and pictures, a logical sequence of events, and a balance of text and pictures throughout story.

- Intermediate—student creates an autobiography that has a well-designed cover with relevant text and pictures, a balance of milestones and minor events, and appropriately captioned pictures and photos.

Informational Brochure: Student for Hire

These rubrics assess students' use of the five-step writing process to produce an informational brochure promoting a service the student can provide (lawn mowing, babysitting, etc.). The goal, or highest degree of accomplishment on the rubric, for each grade level follows:

- Primary—student creates a brochure that has an illustrated cover with at least one color picture, an accurate account of services and fees, and accurate contact information.

- Intermediate—student creates a brochure that has an illustrated cover with full-color graphics, an accurate and appealing account of services and fees, and accurate contact information.

Letter: Keep in Touch

These rubrics assess students' use of the five-step writing process to compose a letter and envelope. The goal, or highest degree of accomplishment on the rubric, for each grade level follows:

- Primary—the student composes a letter that has four or five sentences, a salutation and closing, an effective topic sentence, no mechanical errors, and a correctly addressed envelope.

- Intermediate—the student composes a letter that has six to eight sentences, an error-free salutation and closing, an effective topic sentence that unifies the letter, no mechanical errors, and a correctly addressed envelope.

How to Use the
FICTION Rubric
at the Primary Level

Introduce the Rubric

Distribute and discuss the rubric with students before they begin writing a story. Review terms, including *plot, character, setting,* and *theme,* providing concrete examples to make sure students understand their meanings. Discuss the concepts of logical plot sequence, believable character behavior, a well-described story setting, and a theme that relates to story events. Review the rubric column that contains the highest degree of mastery so that students understand that they must achieve these objectives to receive full credit. Incorporate the five-step process into the assignment, allowing time for each step.

Make the Assignment

Instruct students to write a story about a character they have created doing whatever they want him or her to do. The idea here is for students to write a story about someone other than themselves and have that person do something that the author might not have the opportunity or ability to do. For example, a student might make up a story about a person who flew to Mars in a 1969 Mustang. The student author should control the variables in the story and be restricted only by the need for a beginning (taking off from Earth), middle (arriving on Mars), and ending (returning to Earth). At this level, students can write stories of one to two pages.

Assess Student Understanding

Plot
■ devises logical plot sequence

Character
■ creates believable character behavior

Setting
■ describes setting well

WRITING   **FICTION**   PRIMARY

Task: Student will use the five-step writing process to compose a short work of fiction.

Goal/Standard: Demonstrate understanding of interaction of plot, character, setting, and theme

Criteria	2	1	0	Total Points
Plot	Logical sequence	Illogical sequence	Undeveloped	____ x 5 = ____ points
Character	Believable behavior	Inconsistent behavior	Undeveloped	____ x 5 = ____ points
Setting	Well described	Poor description	Undeveloped	____ x 5 = ____ points
Theme	Clear and relevant to plot events	Not well developed	Not present	____ x 5 = ____ points

37–40 = A
35–36 = B
31–34 = C   Total score ____ /40 = ____
28–30 = D
<28 = F

Theme

■ uses theme relevant to plot events

Keep the assessment rubric available while you read the completed story. If you withhold points, refer, in writing or during a conference with the student, to specific passages in the story that reflect an inability to understand the criteria listed in the rubric. Offer a concrete example to demonstrate what you expected relating to a particular criterion. Logical sequence is a chain of story events that follow a recognizable order rather than jumping from Point A to Point C then back to Point B. A believable character can have two heads as long as the creature's feelings are relevant to the reader's, such as feelings of loneliness (during the long trip to Mars) or fear of the unknown (life-forms that may live on Mars). A setting may be light years from our universe, but readers should be able to close their eyes and imagine how it feels to be in that place. If the theme of the story is "conquering your fears" and the main character never encounters anything fearsome, the story falls short of expressing its theme.

How to Use the
FICTION Rubric
at the Intermediate Level

Introduce the Rubric

Distribute and discuss the rubric with students before they begin writing a story. At this level, students have had considerable exposure to fiction, and most are familiar with the structure of a simple story. Focus on the column of the rubric that contains the highest degree of performance, providing concrete examples of a balance of major and minor plot events, character behavior and story setting that have relevance to the plot, and a clear and adequate underlying message, or theme. Make sure students understand that they must achieve the objectives in the highest-performance column to receive full credit. Incorporate the five-step process into the assignment, allowing time for each step.

Make the Assignment

Students at this level can produce a story of three to seven pages. Tell students the story should contain at least two or three characters. (You can decide and inform students whether you will base the rubric requirements on the main character only or on all characters.) Because students have had exposure to various types of literature, you may want to assign a specific type of story, such as a fantasy, a mystery, or science fiction. Although these stories have the basic elements of fiction in common, they have very different characters and settings, and emerging authors will enjoy experimenting with the various choices.

Assess Student Understanding

Plot
- balance of major and minor events

Character
- believable characters with predictable response to story conflict

Setting
- vivid setting relevant to plot

WRITING  INTERMEDIATE

Task: Student will use the five-step writing process to compose a short work of fiction.

Goal/Standard: Demonstrate understanding of interaction of plot, character, setting, and theme

Criteria	4	3	2	1	Total Points
Plot	Balance of major and minor events	Good plot, logical sequence	Adequate	Sequence not always logical	____ × 5 = ____ points
Character	Predictable response to story problem	Believable behavior	Inconsistent behavior	Not always believable	____ × 5 = ____ points
Setting	Vivid and relevant to plot events	Good description	Adequate description	Poor description	____ × 5 = ____ points
Theme	Clear and relevant message	Relevant to plot events	Adequate underlying message	Not well developed	____ × 5 = ____ points

74–80 = A
70–73 = B
62–69 = C
56–61 = D
<56 = F

Total score ____/80 = ____

Theme

■ clear and relevant message

Keep the assessment rubric at hand while you read the completed story. If you withhold points, refer, in writing or during a conference with the student, to specific passages in the story that reflect an inability to understand the criteria listed in the rubric. Be prepared to provide a concrete alternative example to clarify student thinking. A well-balanced tale contains a major event that drives the character response and story action, and minor events that bring the story and character to life by filling in the blanks about characters. The minor events offer readers a glimpse of how the character reacts in a variety of situations, thus allowing readers to predict how that character will react to the major event in the story. The setting should exist to enhance the plot and character by providing background that can bring out the best (and worst) in characters as they move from one scene to another. The theme should be relevant to readers because it provides the main reason authors write a story.

How to Use the
GREETING CARD Rubric
at the Primary Level

Introduce the Rubric

Distribute and discuss the rubric with students before they begin making a greeting card. Although students at this level have probably made greetings for parents and grandparents, they may be unfamiliar with the particulars of the greeting card format: cover illustration, cover text, and inside message. Provide a sample in class while discussing the rubric criteria, noting how the use of color and an overall neat appearance enhance greeting cards. Be sure students know what you expect of them and understand that they must meet the objectives in the highest-performance column of the rubric to receive full credit. Incorporate the five-step process into the assignment, allowing time for each step.

Make the Assignment

Instruct students to assemble any supplies, such as scissors, crayons, and markers, before they begin their greeting card. The cards may be a class project or an individual project to celebrate a specific occasion. Use this opportunity to talk about some words students might use for the greeting and write those words on the board. Instruct students to write their greetings on a "sloppy copy" first and check with a peer editor, the dictionary, and you to make sure everything is accurate. Once they have checked the greeting for accuracy, provide students with the greeting card paper.

Assess Student Understanding

Cover Design
- two or three colors

Content
- appropriate message with no errors

Overall Appearance
- neat cover; no misspellings

Keep the rubric available while reviewing the card. Because the cards are likely heading for a destination beyond the classroom, show students their errors and give them an opportunity to correct them.

GREETING CARD

Task: Student will use the five-step writing process to create a greeting card.

Goal/Standard: Demonstrate understanding with occasion-appropriate greeting card

Criteria	2	1	0	Total Points
Cover design	2 or 3 colors	Pencil sketch	No artwork	____ x 3 = ____ points
Content	Appropriate message with no errors	Inappropriate message	None	____ x 3 = ____ points
Overall appearance	Neat cover; no misspellings	Neat cover; some misspellings	Poor illustrations; many misspellings	____ x 4 = ____ points

19–20 = A
18 = B
16–17 = C
14–15 = D
<14 = F

Total score ____/20 = ____

How to Use the
GREETING CARD Rubric
at the Intermediate Level

Introduce the Rubric

Distribute and discuss the rubric with students before they begin making a greeting card. Students at this level have had some experience in making bifold and quarter-fold greeting cards, so you can review these techniques quickly. Focus on the column of the rubric that contains the highest degree of performance, reminding students that they must achieve these objectives to receive full credit. Incorporate the five-step process into the assignment, allowing time for each step.

Make the Assignment

Students at this level have been making greeting cards for some time and understand that the cover design should relate to the message inside the card. To reinforce this concept, provide some commercial or handmade samples. If students are making the cards to commemorate a particular occasion, such as Father's Day or Valentine's Day, spend some time discussing words they might use in the message and write these words on the board. Instruct students to assemble their materials, such as scissors, crayons, and markers, before they begin their cards. Remind them to write their message on a "sloppy copy" and check it for spelling, grammatical, and punctuation errors before transferring it to the card. Once the card's message is accurate, provide students with the greeting card paper.

Assess Student Understanding

Cover Design
- full-color illustration

Content
- creative language appropriate to occasion

Overall Appearance
- excellent quality

Keep the rubric available while reviewing the card. Because the cards are likely destined for a location beyond the classroom, review errors with students and provide students time to correct their mistakes.

WRITING **GREETING CARD** INTERMEDIATE

Task: Student will use the five-step writing process to create a greeting card.

Goal/Standard: Demonstrate understanding with occasion-appropriate greeting card

Giving 0 points is an option—no evidence, no credit.

Criteria	4	3	2	1	Total Points
Cover design	Full-color illustration	2 or 3 colors	1 color	Pencil sketch	____ × 3 = ____ points
Content	Creative language appropriate to occasion	Appropriate to occasion	Adequate message	Inappropriate message	____ × 3 = ____ points
Overall appearance	Excellent quality	Good quality	Neat cover; no misspellings	Neat cover; some misspellings	____ × 4 = ____ points

37–40 = A
35–36 = B
30–35 = C
28–30 = D
<28 = F

Total score ____/40 = ____

How to Use the
AUTOBIOGRAPHY Rubric
at the Primary Level

Introduce the Rubric

Distribute and discuss the rubric with students before they begin to write. Make sure students understand the term *autobiography* and that such an account should match the chronological order of their lives. Focus attention on the rubric column that contains the highest degree of performance, reminding students that they must achieve these objectives to receive full credit. Incorporate the five-step process into the assignment, allowing time for each step.

Make the Assignment

Have students create a prewriting web to organize their information before writing. They will submit this web or outline with their manuscript. Students at this level are capable of writing one page, including pictures and photos, for each year of their lives, relating major events and interesting information about each year in the order events occurred. Instruct students to ask parents or guardians for help sifting through childhood pictures to recall events for possible inclusion in the autobiographical account. They can include small photos or pictures on the page in newspaper-type format.

Assess Student Understanding

Cover Design
■ well designed with text and pictures

Sequence
■ logical order of events

Content
■ appropriate balance of text and pictures or photos

Keep the rubric and outline available while reviewing the account. If the autobiography contains errors in sequence, instruct the student to return to the web or outline to verify the proper order in which events occurred. This assessment focuses on appropriate format and length.

AUTOBIOGRAPHY

Task: Student will use the five-step writing process to compile an autobiography with text and pictures.

Goal/Standard: Demonstrate understanding with completion of autobiography

Criteria	2	1	0	Total Points
Cover design	Well designed with text and pictures	Text only	None	_____ x 3 = _____ points
Sequence	Logical order of events	Omissions and reversals	None	_____ x 3 = _____ points
Overall appearance	Appropriate balance of text and pictures or photos	Text with few pictures or photos	Poor organization; all text or all pictures	_____ x 4 = _____ points

19–20 = A
18 = B
16–17 = C
14–15 = D
<14 = F

Total score _____/20 = _____

How to Use the
AUTOBIOGRAPHY Rubric
at the Intermediate Level

Introduce the Rubric

Distribute and discuss the rubric with students before they begin to write. Focus attention on the rubric column that contains the highest degree of performance, reminding students that they must achieve these objectives to receive full credit. Review the importance of sequence in an autobiography as well as the need to include some supporting details to energize the life story. Incorporate the five-step process into the assignment, allowing time for each step.

Make the Assignment

Prewriting webs and outlines help students organize the information about their lives and decide which information to include in the autobiography. Instruct students to seek help from parents or guardians, collecting photos to recall important events for possible inclusion in the autobiography. Students at this level are capable of writing approximately one page for each early (preschool) year of their lives and one to two pages for school years.

Assess Student Understanding

Cover Design
- well designed with relevant text and pictures

Sequence
- sequence of major events enhanced with minor events

Content
- inclusion of appropriately captioned photos or pictures

Keep the assessment rubric available while reviewing the account. Have students who experience difficulty with the sequencing aspect of autobiographical writing refer to their web or outline to clarify the order of events. Make sure that all photos and pictures in the account contain appropriate, explanatory captions or commentary to help readers understand why the author included them.

AUTOBIOGRAPHY

Task: Student will use the five-step writing process to compile an autobiography with text and pictures.

Goal/Standard: Demonstrate understanding with completion of autobiography

Criteria	4	3	2	1	Total Points
Cover design	Well designed with relevant text and pictures	Relevant text and pictures	Text and pictures	Text only	____ × 3 = ____ points
Sequence	Sequence of major events enhanced with minor events	Includes only major events	Logical order of events	Omissions and reversals	____ × 3 = ____ points
Content	Inclusion of appropriately captioned photos or pictures	Appropriate balance of text with pictures or photos	Text with few pictures or photos	Text only; no pictures	____ × 4 = ____ points

37–40 = A
35–36 = B
30–34 = C
28–30 = D
<28 = F

Total score ____/40 = ____

How to Use the

INFORMATIONAL BROCHURE Rubric

at the Primary Level

Introduce the Rubric

Distribute and discuss the rubric with students before they begin work on the brochure. Brochures of this type can advertise services the student can offer (dog walking, car washing) or announce an upcoming event in the student's life, such as an important sporting or artistic competition. Discuss reasons students might create a brochure and why they should arrange the information in a reader-friendly format. Provide concrete examples of informational brochures to allow students to examine brochures' arrangement of information. Focus attention on the rubric column that contains the highest degree of performance, making sure students understand that they must achieve these objectives to receive full credit. Incorporate the five-step process into the assignment, allowing time for each step.

Make the Assignment

Help students decide which information to share on the brochure. Discuss a variety of household chores, such as car washing or garden weeding, they could perform for family and friends. Simply having students create brochures and then leave them in class is not as meaningful as a performance task of having students distribute the brochures in the real world. Make sure parents or guardians are aware of the services the student is offering and agree with the arrangement. Discuss the need to include information about how people interested in the service can contact the student. Have students use a web to organize the information and to make sure they include everything before they transfer the information to a bifold or trifold brochure.

Assess Student Understanding

Cover Design

- text and at least one-color picture

Description of Services

- present and accurate

INFORMATIONAL BROCHURE

Task: Student will use the five-step writing process to produce an informational brochure promoting a service the student can provide.

Goal/Standard: Demonstrate understanding with completed brochure

Criteria	2	1	0	Total Points
Cover design	Text and at least one-color picture	Text only	None	____ x 3 = ____ points
Description of services	Present and accurate	Present with omissions	None	____ x 3 = ____ points
Contact information	Present and accurate	Present with omissions	None	____ x 4 = ____ points

19–20 = A
18 = B
16–17 = C
14–15 = D
<14 = F

Total score ____/20 = ____

Contact Information

- present and accurate

Keep the assessment rubric available while reviewing the brochure. Note the arrangement of information in a bifold or trifold format and its ease of use for readers. At this level, the cover graphic can be a drawing. Make sure students describe the services they are offering realistically in light of their age and level of ability. For example, it is unlikely that an 8-year-old would be able to walk a large, powerful dog, such as a husky or a shepherd.

How to Use the

INFORMATIONAL BROCHURE Rubric

at the Intermediate Level

Introduce the Rubric

Distribute and discuss the assessment rubric with students before they begin work on the brochure. Focus attention on the rubric column that contains the highest degree of performance, making sure students understand that they must achieve these objectives to receive full credit. Make sure students understand that they must be able to stand behind the services or announcement the brochure describes. For example, if the student offers to weed the garden of a customer, the student must be willing and able to complete that task. If the brochure advertises an upcoming sporting event the student is taking part in, the information about the time and location of the event must be accurate. Incorporate the five-step process into the assignment, allowing time for each step.

Make the Assignment

Place students in small groups and have them brainstorm services or announcements they might place in the brochure. Remind them of the importance of an accurate and complete account of the services they are offering. For example, if a student offers lawn-mowing services, the student must consider whether the customers will provide mowers and lawn bags. This type of information helps customers make decisions about using such services. Ask them to consider which illustrations or graphics might enhance the brochure. In some instances, students may wish to work together on a brochure to offer a service jointly, such as a two-person lawn-mowing service. In those instances, check with students throughout the process to make sure both students offer input for the creation of the brochure. Discuss the importance of accurate contact information so parties interested in their services can contact them, and remind students to share the "sloppy copy" of their descriptions of services with you and with peer editors to check for clear and accurate content. Many computer software packages offer step-by-step guides for preparing a professional-quality brochure, and students at this level can use software successfully with minimal teacher assistance.

WRITING **INFORMATIONAL BROCHURE** INTERMEDIATE

Task: Student will use the five-step writing process to produce an informational brochure promoting a service the student can provide (lawn mowing, babysitting, etc.).

Goal/Standard: Demonstrate understanding with completed brochure

Criteria	4	3	2	1	Total Points
Cover design	Text, graphics, and pictures in full color	Text, graphics, and pictures in black and white	Text and graphics	Text only	____ × 3 = ____ points
Description of services	Complete, accurate, and appealing	Complete and accurate	Complete with inaccuracies	Present with omissions	____ × 3 = ____ points
Contact information	Complete, accurate, and well-positioned	Complete and accurate	Complete with inaccuracies	Present with omissions	____ × 4 = ____ points

37–40 = A
35–36 = B
31–34 = C
28–30 = D
<28 = F

Total score ____/40 = ____

Assess Student Understanding

Cover Design
- text, graphics, and pictures in full color

Description of Services
- complete, accurate, and appealing

Contact Information
- complete, accurate, and well-positioned

Keep the assessment rubric available while reviewing the brochure. Make sure the brochure offers an accurate and reader-friendly account of the type of services or the announcement featured. Make sure that contact information is accurate and easy for potential customers to locate.

How to Use the
LETTER Rubric
at the Primary Level

Introduce the Rubric

Distribute and discuss the rubric with students before they begin composing a letter. Discuss the purpose and different types of letters along with how important it is that letter writers make their thoughts clear because they will not be present to offer a detailed explanation to letter recipients. Focus attention on the rubric column that contains the highest degree of performance, making sure students understand that they must achieve these objectives to receive full credit. Review the parts of a letter, including the salutation and closing, and provide a concrete example of the proper arrangement of a completed letter on a page. Incorporate the five-step process into the assignment, allowing time for each step.

Make the Assignment

Students should write to someone they do not know with a specific request. For example, they may wish to write letters to a favorite author with questions about his or her work or to a zookeeper with questions about animal care. Instruct students to decide who will receive their letters and what they want to ask before they begin writing the letter. Students at this level can produce a four- to five-sentence letter. Discuss the importance of the topic sentence, which lets the reader know almost immediately what the letter's author is talking about and sets the tone for the communication. Have students write the message on a "sloppy copy" to give to their peers to check during the editing step for spelling, grammar, and punctuation errors before they transfer it to better-quality stationery. Make sure students know the full address of the recipient, including zip code, before providing them with an envelope.

Assess Student Understanding

Salutation and Closing
- two elements present

Topic Sentence
- present and effective

LETTER

Task: Student will use the five-step writing process to compose and send a letter.

Goal/Standard: Demonstrate understanding with completed letter and envelope

Criteria	2	1	0	Total Points
Salutation and closing	2 elements present	1 element present	None	____ x 3 = ____ points
Topic sentence	Present and effective	Present but not effective	None	____ x 4 = ____ points
Body of letter	4 to 5 sentences; no errors	4 or 5 sentences; few errors	4 to 5 sentences; many errors	____ x 4 = ____ points
Envelope	Accurate and complete	Present with omissions	None	____ x 4 = ____ points

19–20 = A
18 = B
16–17 = C
14–15 = D
<14 = F

Total score ____ /30 = ____

Body of Letter

■ four or five sentences; no errors

Envelope

■ accurate and complete

Keep the assessment rubric available while reviewing the letter. It is likely that the letter is destined for a location beyond the classroom, so review any errors with students and give them a chance to make corrections before sending the letter. Consider giving students an extra credit point if they receive a reply to their letter.

How to Use the
LETTER Rubric
at the Intermediate Level

Introduce the Rubric

Distribute and discuss the rubric with students before they begin composing a letter. Discuss the purpose of letters and the need for their letters to request information in a way that makes the recipient happy to respond. Review the parts of a letter, including the salutation and closing, and provide a concrete example of the proper arrangement of a completed letter on a page. Focus attention on the rubric column that contains the highest degree of performance, reminding students that they must achieve these objectives to receive full credit. Incorporate the five-step process into the assignment, allowing time for each step.

Make the Assignment

With students working in pairs or triads, have them discuss who will receive their letters. The letters should request information from someone they do not know, and the tone of the letters should reflect students' reason for making contact with the letter's recipient. Recipients can be anyone from a favorite author to a local business owner as long as the student is able to locate a name and accurate contact information. Have students draft their letters of six to eight sentences on a "sloppy copy" to give to their peers to check during the editing step for spelling, grammar, and punctuation errors before they transfer the message to appropriate stationery. During the revising phase, students reading the letter to their revision group could solicit comments about what the group thinks the letter is requesting. Have each student confirm the full mailing address of the letter's recipient before providing them with an envelope.

Assess Student Understanding

Salutation and Closing
- two appropriate elements present with no errors

Topic Sentence
- sentence that unifies letter

LETTER

Task: Student will use the five-step writing process to compose and send a letter.

Goal/Standard: Demonstrate understanding with completed letter and envelope

Criteria	4	3	2	1	Total Points
Salutation and closing	2 appropriate elements present with no errors	Both elements present but 1 or both inappropriate	2 elements present with some errors	1 element present	____ × 3 = ____ points
Topic sentence	Sentence that unifies letter	Present, accurate, and effective	Present and accurate but not effective	Present but ungrammatical	____ × 3 = ____ points
Body of letter	6 to 8 sentences with no errors	6 to 8 sentences with few errors	4 to 5 sentences with no errors	4 to 5 sentences with few errors	____ × 5 = ____ points
Envelope	Complete and accurate	Complete with 1 or 2 misspellings	Some inaccuracies	Present with omissions	____ × 4 = ____ points

56–60 = A
52–55 = B
47–51 = C
42–46 = D
<42 = F

Total score ____/60 = ____

Body of Letter

■ six to eight sentences with no errors

Envelope

■ complete and accurate

Keep the assessment rubric available while reviewing the letter. Make sure the letter meets the stated purpose of requesting information from a recipient whom the letter writer does not know. The letter is likely destined for a location beyond the classroom, so review any errors with students and allow them to make corrections before mailing the letters.

Assessment Rubrics and Oral Language

6

To prepare her students for the challenges of middle school, intermediate-level teacher Michelle designs and teaches a wide variety of oral language activities in her social studies classes. Reflecting on the types of classroom exercises and extracurricular experiences (oral reports, debates, theater, storytelling) her students will face in the years ahead, Michelle develops assessment rubrics for each type of activity. She shares these rubrics with her students as they participate in each exercise. By creating these forms of assessment, Michelle enables her students to take control of their performance by focusing on strengths and weaknesses in each area of oral language presentation.

ORAL PRESENTATIONS

Michelle's students are fortunate that she invests time and energy to help them maximize their future school experience. In many cases, grade-school teachers assess students' oral performances solely on content, disregarding such categories as eye contact and enunciation. When students move into the upper grades and are judged on these and other presentation-related skills, their limited prior experience often makes them self-conscious about giving speeches or engaging in debates. Their reluctance can escalate if students remain confused about what they are doing incorrectly. Michelle's efforts to help students identify and refine their public speaking skills will yield positive effects in the lives of these students long after they have moved beyond classroom walls into the real world.

The rubrics in this chapter cover four areas related to oral language skills: storytelling, dramatic presentation, oral reporting, and debate. These rubrics list full-credit responses to provide teachers with concrete examples of what they may see in student work. A summary of expectations for each age and grade level follows. For areas not suitable for primary grades, no rubric appears at that level.

Storytelling: It's Story Time!

These rubrics assess students' ability to tell a fictional story with props or costumes. The goal, or highest degree of accomplishment on the rubric, for each grade level follows:

- Primary—student selects story appropriate for intended audience, tells story with no omissions or reversals in story sequence, and uses adequate vocal tone and pace and appropriate props or costumes.

- Intermediate—student selects story that encourages audience interaction with storyteller, emphasizes major events in story sequence, and uses vocal inflection and props or costumes that enhance retelling.

Dramatic Presentation: The Play's the Thing

These rubrics assess students' participation in a dramatic presentation. The goal, or highest degree of accomplishment on the rubric, for each grade level follows:

- Primary—student has vocal delivery, gestures, and movements appropriate for characters and story and uses props and costumes relevant to the story.

- Intermediate—student uses vocal delivery that engages audience attention and interest, gestures and movements that enhance verbal delivery, and props and costumes that provide additional information about character.

Oral Report: What's News?

These rubrics assess students' ability to present an oral news report with visual aids. The goal, or highest degree of accomplishment on the rubric, for each grade level follows:

- Primary—student addresses and organizes topic adequately, speaks with adequate volume and pace, looks at notes and at audience, and uses adequately constructed, relevant visual aids.

- Intermediate—student addresses and organizes topic well, speaks with appropriate emphasis, maintains eye contact with audience, and uses well-constructed, relevant visual aids.

Debates: That's Debatable

These rubrics assess students' participation in a formal or informal debate. The goal, or highest degree of accomplishment on the rubric, for the intermediate level follows: Student speaks in a well-modulated voice, stays focused on debate topic, maintains eye contact with audience and opponent(s), and observes debating rules.

How to Use the
STORYTELLING Rubric
at the Primary Level

Introduce the Rubric

Distribute and discuss the rubric with students before they begin the activity. Focus attention on the column containing the highest level of performance, reminding students that to receive full credit they must achieve these objectives. Make sure students understand the difference between storytelling and reading aloud. Unlike the reader, a storyteller must know the story with little or no aid from index cards or other cuing devices.

Make the Assignment

Students at this level might tell incredible stories due to their unbridled imaginations. For this assignment, however, it is important that their stories have a clear beginning, middle, and ending. Begin by having students retell one of their favorite stories from a work of children's literature. They can refer to the book as a guide while practicing their retelling, and teachers can recognize almost immediately if gaps or reversals occur in the story sequence. Set time guidelines (3 to 6 minutes) to help students who might stray from the purpose of telling the story. Props and costumes are an excellent way to enhance the retelling and give storytellers something on which to build their storyteller persona. Discuss the types of props students can use, such as hats, shawls, or puppets, and limit students at this level to one to two props or costume items.

Assess Student Understanding

Selection
- appropriate for audience

Sequence
- no omissions or reversals in sequence

Vocal Delivery
- adequate tone and pace

Props or Costumes
- neat and appropriate

ORAL LANGUAGE **STORYTELLING** PRIMARY

Task: Student will tell a fictional story with props or costumes, or both.

Goal/Standard: Performance meets stated criteria.

Criteria	2	1	0	Total Points
Selection	Appropriate for intended audience	Not appropriate for audience	Too long or complex for retelling	____ x 5 = ____ points
Sequence	No omissions or reversals in retelling	Omissions and reversals in retelling	Illogical	____ x 5 = ____ points
Vocal delivery	Adequate tone and pace	Erratic tone and pace	Flat or inaudible tone	____ x 5 = ____ points
Props or costumes	Neat and appropriate	Sloppy; not relevant	None	____ x 5 = ____ points

37–40 = A
35–36 = B
31–34 = C
28–30 = D
<28 = F

Total score ____/40 = ____

Because you will conduct the assessment during the retelling, keep the rubric at hand during that time. Join other audience members in the story circle because, unlike reading aloud, storytellers use their voice as a tool in the retelling and may choose to use a soft voice at times to heighten suspense in a particular part of the story. Know the story beforehand. If you permit students to tell an original story, have a hard copy available to check for omissions or reversals in the sequence. Any story that is of interest to the specific age group is appropriate. For example, a fairy tale is generally appropriate for primary-level storytelling. Props and costumes should enhance not detract from the retelling.

How to Use the

STORYTELLING Rubric

at the Intermediate Level

Introduce the Rubric

Distribute and discuss the rubric with students before they begin the activity. Focus attention on the column containing the highest level of performance, reminding students that to receive full credit they must achieve these objectives. Make sure students understand the difference between storytelling and reading aloud. Unlike the reader, a storyteller must know the story with little or no aid from index cards or other cuing devices.

Make the Assignment

Students at this level are capable of telling stories with multiple characters. They can retell a popular children's story or compose a tale of their own. If they choose the latter, make sure you receive a hard copy of the story so during assessment you can determine whether any omissions or reversals occur. Set time guidelines (5 to 8 minutes) to help storytellers focus on telling only the story without venturing into asides that may detract from the tale. Instruct students to select a tale appropriate for their audience and one that gets the audience actively involved in the retelling through such devices as repetition of certain lines or gestures. So you can assess their ability to emphasize major events, instruct them to select a story with three or four major events and one or two minor details to go with each event. Discuss the types of props they can use, such as hats, shawls, or puppets, but limit students at this level to two or three props or costume items.

Assess Student Understanding

Selection

■ encourages audience interaction with storyteller

Sequence

■ emphasizes major story events

Vocal Delivery

■ uses appropriate vocal inflection

ORAL LANGUAGE   **STORYTELLING**   INTERMEDIATE

Task: Student will tell a fictional story using props and/or costumes.

Goal/Standard: Performance meets stated criteria.

Criteria	4	3	2	1	Total Points
Selection	Encourages audience interaction with storyteller	Appropriate for audience in content and length	Appropriate for audience but too long	Not appropriate for audience	____ x 5 = ____ points
Sequence	Emphasizes major story events	No omissions or reversals in retelling	1 or 2 omissions and reversals in retelling	Difficult to follow	____ x 5 = ____ points
Vocal delivery	Uses appropriate vocal inflection	Good, even tone and pace	Adequate tone and pace	Erratic tone and pace	____ x 5 = ____ points
Props or costumes	Enhance retelling	Neat and appropriate	Present but do not enhance story	Sloppy or not relevant	____ x 5 = ____ points

74–80 = A
62–69 = C
70–73 = B
56–61 = D
<56 = F

Total score ____ /80 = ____

Props or Costumes
- enhance the retelling

Because you will conduct the assessment during the retelling, keep the rubric at hand during that time. Join other audience members in the story circle because, unlike reading aloud, storytellers use their voices as a tool in the retelling and may choose to use a soft voice at times to heighten suspense in a particular part of the story. Know the story beforehand. Again, if you permit students to tell an original story, keep a hard copy available to check for omissions or reversals in the sequence. Any story that is of interest to the specific age group is appropriate. Intermediate-level storytellers gravitate toward stories of people in their age group. Look for the storyteller's emphasis on major events. Props and costumes should enhance not detract from the retelling.

How to Use the

DRAMATIC PRESENTATION Rubric

at the Primary Level

Introduce the Rubric

Distribute and discuss the rubric with students before they begin the activity. Focus attention on the column containing the highest level of performance, reminding students that to receive full credit they must achieve those objectives. Review the criteria for dramatic performance, including use of voice and gestures to create a memorable character, making sure students understand the difference between this type of exercise and other oral presentations, such as show-and-tell or an oral report.

Make the Assignment

Students at this level are capable of memorizing a small amount of dialogue (fewer than 10 lines) in preparation for their appearance in a dramatic presentation. The play can be teacher composed or a published play suitable for the grade level. (Suitable published plays are available in libraries or through children's magazines.) Students can work together as a group on a play. For example, one student might take the role of an adult who does not know which career to follow. One by one, the other students in the class tell their classmate, the high school student, about their chosen profession. Each character may have only a few lines, but the entire play might take about 15 to 20 minutes because the entire class participates.

Before the dramatic performance activity, make sure students know their lines well so they focus on effective delivery and do not simply recite the dialogue. Although most students at this level do not possess the ability to display a wide range of emotions in the context of a dramatic presentation, they are able to act happy or sad based on the nature of their character's situation. Ask students what they do when they are happy or sad or frightened or embarrassed and have them show you by using their hands, arms, and face. If they perform the play before an audience other than their classmates, provide time for students to prepare their lines and practice delivery, preferably in a room comparable with the one housing the actual performance. As the class makes preparations for the play, hold a group discussion about props and costumes that would work with each character. Solicit help from parents or friends in acquiring the props necessary for the play.

Assess Student Understanding

Vocal Delivery
- ■ appropriate tone and pace for character

Gestures and Movements
- ■ appropriate for character

Props or Costumes
- ■ present and relevant to story

Because the assessment will take place during the dramatic presentation, keep the rubric at hand during that time. Students should speak in a clear voice so audience members can hear them, pacing their lines to convey the intended emotion. Observe how students use hand and facial gestures as well as how they move about the performance area. Note whether these gestures and movements are consistent with the character. For example, if the character is supposed to be happy, gestures and movements should convey that emotion. Note whether costumes or any props the student uses are consistent with the character and do not distract the audience from the performer's words or actions.

ORAL LANGUAGE   # DRAMATIC PRESENTATION   PRIMARY

Task: Student will participate in a dramatic presentation.

Goal/Standard: Performance meets stated criteria.

Criteria	2	1	0	Total Points
Vocal delivery	Appropriate tone and pace for character	Lacks expression; barely audible tone	Forgets lines; inaudible tone	_____ x 4 = _____ points
Gestures and movements	Appropriate for character	Stilted and unnatural	None	_____ x 3 = _____ points
Props or costumes	Present and relevant to story	Present but not related to story	None	_____ x 3 = _____ points

19–20 = A
18 = B
16–17 = C
14–15 = D
<14 = F

Total score _____/20 = _____

How to Use the

DRAMATIC PRESENTATION
Rubric

at the Intermediate Level

Introduce the Rubric

Distribute and discuss the rubric with students before they begin the activity. Focus attention on the column containing the highest level of performance, reminding students that to receive full credit they must achieve those objectives. Review the criteria for dramatic performance, including use of voice and gestures to create a memorable character, making sure students understand the difference between this type of exercise and other oral presentations, such as show-and-tell or an oral report.

Make the Assignment

Students at this level are capable of memorizing a moderate amount of dialogue (10 to 20 lines) in preparation for their appearance in a dramatic presentation. The play can be teacher composed or a published play suitable for the grade level. (Suitable published plays are available in libraries or through children's magazines.) Students can work together as a group on a play.

Before the oral performance activity, make sure students know their lines well so they can focus on effective delivery and do not simply recite the dialogue. Although some students at this level do not possess the ability to display a wide range of emotions in the context of a dramatic presentation, most students are able to act happy or sad based on the nature of their character's situation. (You may want to prompt them by asking them what they do when they feel happy or sad or embarrassed or surprised and so on.) In the area of props and costumes, talk to students about the character and what he or she might do with a particular article of clothing. A shady person might try to use a cape to obscure his facial features, and a proud person might continually fluff her dress to make it look more pleasing. If they are to perform before an audience other than their classmates, provide time for students to prepare their lines and practice delivery, preferably in a room comparable with the one housing the actual performance.

ORAL LANGUAGE   **DRAMATIC PRESENTATION**   INTERMEDIATE

Task: Student will participate in a dramatic presentation.

Goal/Standard: Performance meets stated criteria.

Criteria	4	3	2	1	Total Points
Vocal delivery	Engages audience attention	Appropriate tone and pace for character	Adequate tone and pace	Forgets lines or lacks expression	____ x 4 = ____ points
Gestures and movements	Enhance verbal delivery	Appropriate for character	Adequate gestures and movement	Stilted or unnatural (overdone)	____ x 3 = ____ points
Props or costumes	Provide information about character	Neat, clever, and relevant to story	Present and relevant to story	Present but not related to story or sloppy	____ x 3 = ____ points

37–40 = A
35–36 = B
31–34 = C
28–30 = D
<28 = F

Total score ____/40 = ____

Assess Student Understanding

Vocal Delivery

- engages audience attention

Gestures and Movements

- enhance verbal delivery

Props or Costumes

- provide information about the character

Because the assessment will take place during the dramatic presentation, keep the rubric at hand during that time. Students should speak clearly so audience members can hear them, pacing their lines to convey the intended emotion. Observe how students use hand and facial gestures as well as how they move about the performance area and determine whether these gestures and movements are consistent with the character. Note whether the costumes or props students use are consistent with the character. These visual aids should offer additional information about the character, such as a bold-colored scarf or hat to identify the character as an outgoing person, but they should not distract the audience from the performer's words or actions.

How to Use the
ORAL REPORT Rubric
at the Primary Level

Introduce the Rubric

Distribute and discuss the rubric with students before they begin their oral reports. Focus attention on the rubric column containing the highest levels of performance, reminding students that to receive full credit they must achieve these objectives. Students at this level can handle some reporting of factual information, although the majority of student presentations will focus on students' ideas and opinions.

Make the Assignment

Students at this level can engage in such oral reports as show-and-tell or group or circle sharing time. Their participation in these activities should follow the guidelines in the rubric because these primary activities are the foundation for future oral presentations. For early primary grades, begin with a simple show-and-tell presentation. Older primary students (Grades 2 and 3) may feel more comfortable with a group or circle time activity when they can share an event they experienced, such as a special vacation or celebration. Set a time limit, approximately 3 to 5 minutes, to help students plan their presentations more effectively. To enhance the presentation for visual learners, instruct students to bring a relevant visual aid to accompany their oral report. (This instruction is not necessary for show-and-tell if students bring an item to share with classmates.)

Assess Student Understanding

Vocal Delivery
- adequate volume and pace

Content
- addresses and organizes topic adequately

Eye Contact
- looks at notes and at audience

Visual Aids
- adequately constructed and relevant

ORAL LANGUAGE　　　　　**ORAL REPORT**　　　　　PRIMARY

Task: Student will present an oral news report with visual aids.

Goal/Standard: Oral report meets stated criteria.

Giving 0 points is an option—no evidence, no credit.

Criteria	2	1	0	Total Points
Vocal delivery	Adequate volume and pace	Erratic volume and/or pace	Inaudible	____ x 5 = ____ points
Content	Addresses and organizes topic adequately	Some weak links in connecting ideas	Unclear topic and report organization	____ x 5 = ____ points
Eye contact	Looks at notes and at audience	Infrequent	Little or none	____ x 5 = ____ points
Visual aids	Adequately constructed and relevant	Poorly made	Little or none	____ x 5 = ____ points

37–40 = A
31–34 = C
35–36 = B
28–30 = D
<28 = F

Total score _____/40 = _____

Because you will conduct the assessment during the oral presentation, keep the rubric at hand during that time. Consider the speaker's volume and pace throughout the presentation. An excessively slow or rapid pace diminishes the impact of the speaker's words. Although speakers at this level may need to rely on notes to make the presentation, they should also be able to make eye contact with audience members, preferably while emphasizing an important part of the oral presentation. The visual aid should enhance the presentation and be relevant to the topic and adequately constructed.

How to Use the
ORAL REPORT Rubric
at the Intermediate Level

Introduce the Rubric

Distribute and discuss the rubric with students before they begin the activity. Focus attention on the rubric column containing the highest levels of performance, reminding students that to receive full credit they must achieve these objectives. Although the majority of these presentations will focus on students' ideas and opinions, students at this level are able to present brief informational presentations.

Make the Assignment

Students at this level have taken classes in a number of content area subjects, such as social studies or science, and these areas can provide ample topics for students preparing an oral report. Compile a list of acceptable topics in either of these or other areas (e.g., health, math, art, music), instructing students to select from the list. Students who wish to prepare a report on another topic should share their reasons for choosing that topic as well as demonstrate their ability to gather and present a sufficient amount of relevant material.

Students at this level are capable of presenting a 5- to 10-minute oral report that includes relevant visual aids to clarify and enhance the information presented.

Assess Student Understanding

Vocal Delivery
- uses volume and pace effectively for emphasis

Content
- addresses and organizes topic well

Eye Contact
- maintains eye contact with audience

Visual Aids
- relevant and well made

ORAL LANGUAGE   # ORAL REPORT   INTERMEDIATE

Task: Student will present an oral news report with visual aids.

Goal/Standard: Oral report meets stated criteria.

Giving 0 points is an option—no evidence, no credit.

Criteria	4	3	2	1	Total Points
Vocal delivery	Uses volume and pace for emphasis	Adequate volume and pace	Good, even volume and pace	Erratic volume and pace statements	____ x 5 = ____ points
Content	Addresses and organizes topic well	Clear topic, logical organization	Addresses and organizes topic adequately	Weak links connecting ideas	____ x 5 = ____ points
Eye contact	Maintains eye contact with audience	Looks more at audience than at notes	Looks at notes and at audience	Infrequent	____ x 5 = ____ points
Visual aids	Relevant and well made	Adequately constructed and relevant	Relevant but not well constructed	Poorly made	____ x 5 = ____ points

74–80 = A
62–69 = C
70–73 = B
56–61 = D
<56 = F

Total score ____/80 = ____

Because you will conduct the assessment during the oral presentation, keep the rubric at hand during that time. Reflect on the speaker's volume and pace throughout the presentation. These factors should vary as the student emphasizes important information in the oral report. Students speaking at an excessively slow or rapid pace diminish the impact of their words. Speakers at this level should not need to rely on notes to make the presentation. They should make eye contact with audience members, especially while emphasizing an important part of the oral presentation. Their visual aid should enhance the presentation and be relevant to the topic and well constructed.

How to Use the
DEBATE Rubric
at the Intermediate Level

Introduce the Rubric

Distribute and discuss the rubric with students before they begin the debate, focusing attention on the column that contains the highest level of performance. Remind students that to receive full credit they must achieve the objectives listed in this column. Use this opportunity to review the rules of debating with students and relate those rules to the objectives in the rubric. For example, debating rules cite the need for debaters to stay on topic, and the rubric mentions this need under the Content heading.

Make the Assignment

Students at this level perform best with a debate format that has a balance of research presentation and student opinions. For example, a debate about the most and least effective solutions to pollution should contain information on studies conducted on that topic as well as some input from students about why they believe certain methods are more or less effective than others. Choose a topic of interest and importance to students. Ask for student input because the more passionately individuals feel about a topic, the more likely they will invest time and energy in researching and presenting a debate. They should conduct their research by reading publications or Internet sites designed for their age group. At this level, have students debate one-on-one or in teams of two students. Set some time limits for presentation (about 1 to 2 minutes per student), rebuttal (about 1 minute per student), and closing arguments (about 3 minutes—in a team format, one student from each team gives the closing argument), and appoint a timekeeper to make sure students adhere to those guidelines. Place the rules of the debate on a checklist, making a copy for each debater.

Assess Student Understanding

Vocal Delivery
■ has well-modulated, clear, and strong delivery

Content
■ stays on topic

ORAL LANGUAGE   # DEBATE   INTERMEDIATE

Task: Student will participate in a formal or informal debate.

Goal/Standard: Debate performance meets stated criteria.

Giving 0 is an option—no evidence, no credit.

Criteria	3	2	1	Total Points
Vocal delivery	Well modulated, clear, and strong	Adequate volume	Erratic volume	____ x 5 = ____ points
Content	Stays on topic	Drifts from topic but catches drift and refocuses	Drifts from topic	____ x 5 = ____ points
Eye contact	Maintains eye contact to connect with audience and opponent(s)	Balances looking at notes with making eye contact	Looks at notes too much	____ x 5 = ____ points
Visual aids	Observes all debate rules	Observes some debate rules	Seems uncertain of debate rules	____ x 5 = ____ points

37–40 = A
31–34 = C
35–36 = B   Total score ____/60 = ____
28–30 = D
<28 = F

Eye Contact

■ maintains eye contact to connect with audience and opponent(s)

Procedure

■ observes all debate rules

Because you will conduct this assessment during the actual debate, keep the rubric at hand during that time. Sit near the back of the room to discover whether the entire audience can hear the debaters' voices. Take note of participants who drift continually from the specified topic and those who read from their notes without looking at their opponent(s) or the audience. During the debate, check those areas where the debater performs at or above age-appropriate expectations as well as those areas where the debater needs improvement.

Rubrics and the Research Process 7

While explaining an upcoming research project to his fifth graders, Peter discovers that a significant number of students lack basic knowledge regarding how to use reference materials and other research tools, such as interviewing or field experiences. Realizing that this deficit would translate into low-quality written reports, Peter opts to shelve the research project until he can remedy the more immediate situation. Before teaching a miniunit on research tools, Peter prepares assessment rubrics for each tool, listing the skills students should possess to use that tool effectively. Creating a rubric before teaching a unit of study offers Peter a chance to reflect on what he wants his students to learn. Sharing these rubrics with the students at the beginning of the unit helps them identify critical skills necessary for conducting research.

INVESTIGATE THE POSSIBILITIES

Each year, as they attempt to prepare their students for middle school, intermediate-level teachers share Peter's discovery that students lack research skills. Knowing how to use research tools effectively is an invaluable skill because it allows student authors to build on their experiences and observations by using the existing body of knowledge on a specific topic. For example, with the topic *wildflowers*, student authors unfamiliar with research tools are limited to their own knowledge about the topic. By using research tools, including a dictionary and an encyclopedia, student authors can gather and include information in their reports about how these natural beauties touch our lives, healing us, feeding us, and creating a more balanced ecosystem. Understanding where to find information and how to incorporate it into oral or written reports are solid first steps in the development of effective research skills.

Although the Internet is an innovative avenue for conducting research, basic materials, such as a dictionary, an encyclopedia, or an atlas, remain tools students can use to compile meaningful research projects.

RESEARCH RUBRICS

The rubrics in this chapter cover the following areas related to good research skills: reference materials, firsthand experiences, written reports, and collaboration. The reference rubrics list required elements in the first column, and teachers note whether a certain behavior is present or absent, while the remaining rubrics in the chapter list full-credit responses to provide teachers with specific examples of what they may see in student work. A summary of the expectations for the age and grade level follows. In cases when students in more than one age- or grade-level group should have all of the skills described, the rubric and assessment guidelines have been combined. In the case of areas not suitable for primary grades, no rubric appears at that level.

Reference Materials: Tools of the Trade

These rubrics assess students' use of reference materials. The goal, or highest degree of accomplishment on the rubric, for each grade level follows:

- Primary—student uses dictionary and encyclopedia guide words to locate words and topics independently and uses an atlas to locate states and countries, capitals, and major cities independently.

- Intermediate—student masters all skills of primary students and understands dictionary abbreviations (for noun, adjective, preposition, etc.), uses a compass rose and map key in an atlas, and distinguishes between major and minor details in encyclopedia entries.

Firsthand Experiences: Let's Make Contact

These rubrics assess students' participation in three information-gathering experiences—a field trip, an interview, and an experiment. The goal, or highest degree of accomplishment on the rubric, for each grade level follows:

- Primary—student records observations during a field trip, asks an interview subject three to five relevant questions, and participates in an experiment or field trial.

- Intermediate—student uses observations and notes from a field trip to formulate questions, uses an interview subject's responses to formulate new questions, and conducts an experiment or field trial.

Written Report: The "Write" Stuff

These rubrics assess students' ability to produce a written research project. The goal, or highest degree of accomplishment on the rubric, for the intermediate level follows: Student responds adequately to topic question, demonstrates grasp of topic's concepts, presents accurate information and proof of accuracy, and prepares an accurate and mostly current bibliography.

Collaboration: Let's Get Together

These rubrics assess students' ability to participate in a collaborative research project. The guidelines for assessment are the same at all levels because the instructions for group work—wait your turn before speaking, hear and respect the opinions of others, complete the tasks assigned to you in the group, and work as a unit to complete the project—are the same no matter what the student age or grade. The goal, or highest degree of accomplishment on the rubric, for intermediate level follows: Student shares information with all group members; makes full eye contact with speakers; asks relevant, open-ended questions; makes encouraging gestures and facial expressions; and distributes tasks logically based on level of difficulty.

How to Use the

REFERENCE MATERIALS
Rubric

at the Primary Level

Introduce the Rubric

Distribute and discuss the rubric with students before they begin the assignment, focusing attention on the column containing the highest level of performance. Remind students that to receive full credit they must achieve these objectives. Because this rubric contains a wide variety of skills, teachers may prefer to conduct a series of activities that specifically test student proficiency with reference materials, rather than simply observe students' use of the materials to complete another assignment.

Make the Assignment

For dictionary skills, provide students with a set of guide words from the top of a page spread in the dictionary, such as *scene* and *seat*, and tell them to list 10 words one can find between those guide words. Next, provide students with a list of five to eight words, instructing them to locate those words in the dictionary within 6 to 10 minutes.

For an atlas, provide students with their own copy of a map and a list of five to eight locations, such as specific states or countries. Number the locations students must identify and instruct them to circle the state or country and write the correct number within the circle. For example, if the third state on the student list is Wyoming, students should be able to circle the state of Wyoming and write a numeral 3 within that circle. Discuss the use of a map key to denote capital and major cities with students. They should be able to distinguish between the symbols representing both types of cities. Next, instruct students to return to their maps and underline the capital city of each circled state or country, and then draw a box around two major cities within that state or country.

For the encyclopedia, provide students with a set of guide words from the encyclopedia, instructing them to list four topics that appear between those guide words. Next, provide students with a list of four topics, instructing them to identify the letter and number of the volume where each topic appears, and then the page number(s) and guide words for the location of the topic.

READING **REFERENCE MATERIALS** PRIMARY

Task: Student will use reference materials to complete assignments.

Goal/Standard: Participation meets stated criteria.

Criteria	2	1	0	Total Points
Dictionary • uses guide words • locates words independently	2 elements present	1 element present	0 elements present	____ x 3 = ____ points
Atlas • locates states or countries • locates capitals and major cities	2 elements present	1 element present	0 elements present	____ x 3 = ____ points
Encyclopedia • uses guide words • locates topics independently	2 elements present	1 element present	0 elements present	____ x 4 = ____ points

19–20 = A
18 = B
16–17 = C
14–15 = D
<14 = F

Total score ____/20 = ____

Assess Student Understanding

Dictionary
- uses guide words
- locates words independently

Have students use the dictionary to check the list of words they created from the guide words you supplied. Errors may be the result of students' misspelling the words on their list. On the timed portion of the activity, reduce the number of words for those students unable to locate every word on the list, gradually working back to the desired number of words within the specified time frame. Dropping back temporarily on the number of words allows students to build up some expertise and experience some success while they gradually work up to the requirements of the original assignment.

Atlas
- locates states or countries
- locates capitals and major cities

Check student maps for accurate responses, reviewing with students the symbols for capital and major cities when necessary. Point out errors and provide time for students to correct their errors until they have 100% accuracy.

Encyclopedia
- uses guide words
- locates topics independently

Provide students with the appropriate encyclopedia volume, instructing them to check their answers. Give credit for a topic that would appear within the guide words but is not contained in the encyclopedia. For example, if a student states that the topic *shoes* appears between encyclopedia guide words *shark* and *skiing,* but the encyclopedia refers users to footwear, the student has still demonstrated the ability to specify topics one might find between those guide words. Next, provide students access to a full set of encyclopedias to check their responses to the second activity. A complete response gives the volume number in which the information appears as well as the page number(s) and guide words where the topic appears.

How to Use the

REFERENCE MATERIALS
Rubric

at the Intermediate Level

Introduce the Rubric

Distribute and discuss the rubric with students before they begin the assignment, focusing attention on the column containing the highest level of performance. Remind students that to receive full credit, they must achieve these objectives. Because this rubric contains a wide variety of skills, teachers may prefer to conduct a series of activities that specifically test student proficiency with reference materials, rather than simply observe students' use of the materials to complete another assignment.

Make the Assignment

For dictionary skills, provide students with a set of guide words from the top of a page spread in the dictionary, such as *scene* and *seat,* and tell them to list 10 words one can find between those guide words. Next, provide students with a list of 8 to 15 words, instructing them to locate those words in the dictionary within 5 to 8 minutes. Finally, make a list of common dictionary abbreviations, instructing students to list the complete term. For example, students should be able to convert */adj/* to *adjective.*

For the atlas, provide students with their own copy of a map and a list of five to eight locations, such as specific states or countries. Number the locations students must identify and instruct them to circle the state or country and write the correct number within the circle. For example, if the third state on the student list is Ohio, students should be able to circle the state of Ohio and write the numeral 3 within that circle. Discuss the use of a map key to denote capital and major cities with students. They should be able to distinguish between the symbols representing both types of cities. Next, instruct students to return to their maps and underline the capital city of each circled state or country and then draw a box around two major cities within that state or country. Finally, provide students with a list of state or country names, instructing them to use the compass rose to identify the states or countries that are north, south, east, and west of each state or country on the list.

For the encyclopedia, provide students with a set of guide words from the encyclopedia, instructing them to list four topics one might find between those guide words. Next, provide students with a list of four topics, instructing them to identify the letter and number of the volume where that topic appears and then give the page number(s) and guide words of the location of the topic. Finally, ask students to explain, in their own words, how they can tell the difference between a major topic and a supporting detail in an encyclopedia entry.

Assess Student Understanding

Dictionary
- uses guide words
- locates words independently
- understands dictionary abbreviations

Have students check their list of words in the dictionary to determine how many of the words appear between the specified guide words. Errors may be the result of students' misspelling the words. On the timed portion of the activity, reduce the number of words for those students unable to locate every word on the list, gradually working back to the desired number of words within the specified time frame. Finally, review student responses for converting dictionary abbreviations to their full-length form. Discuss incorrect responses with students, exploring the reason behind their choices.

Atlas
- locates states or countries
- locates capitals and major cities
- uses compass rose and atlas map key

Check student maps for accurate responses, reviewing the symbols for capital and major cities when necessary. Finally, examine student responses to the compass rose activity. Discuss incorrect responses with students, exploring the reason for their choices.

Encyclopedia
- uses guide words
- locates topic independently
- distinguishes between major and minor details in entry

Provide students with the appropriate encyclopedia volume, instructing them to check their answers. Give credit for a topic that would appear between the guide words but is not in the encyclopedia. For example, if a student states that one might find the topic *shoes* between encyclopedia guide words *shark* and *skiing,* but the encyclopedia refers users to *footwear,* the student has still

RESEARCH **REFERENCE MATERIALS** INTERMEDIATE

Task: Student will use reference materials to complete assignments.

Goal/Standard: Participation meets stated criteria.

Giving 0 points is an option—no evidence, no credit.

Criteria	4	3	2	1	Total Points
Dictionary • uses guide words • locates words independently • understands dictionary abbreviations	3 complete elements present	2 complete elements present	1 complete element present	Evidence of 2+ incomplete elements	____ x 3 = ____ points
Atlas • locates states or countries • locates capitals and major cities • uses compass rose and atlas map key	3 complete elements present	2 complete elements present	1 complete element present	Evidence of 2+ incomplete elements	____ x 3 = ____ points
Encyclopedia • uses guide words • locates topic independently • distinguishes between major and minor details in entry	3 complete elements present	2 complete elements present	1 complete element present	Evidence of 2+ incomplete elements	____ x 4 = ____ points

37–40 = A
35–36 = B
31–34 = C
29–30 = D
<28 = F

Total score ____/40 = ____

demonstrated the ability to specify topics that might appear between those guide words. Next, provide students access to a full set of encyclopedias to check their responses to the second activity. A complete response includes the volume number in which the information appears as well as the page number(s) and guide words associated with that topic. Finally, examine student responses regarding distinguishing between a major topic and a supporting detail in encyclopedia entries. Correct responses may include reference to the typefaces encyclopedias use, such as bold for major topics and italic for sub-headings and details.

How to Use the

FIRSTHAND EXPERIENCE
Rubric

at the Primary Level

Introduce the Rubric

Distribute and discuss the rubric with students before they begin the assignment. Focus attention on the column containing the highest level of performance, reminding students that to receive full credit they must achieve these objectives. This rubric is well suited for a science unit. Because it deals with three different types of firsthand experience—observation, interview, and participation—you need not complete the rubric at a single session but may use it to monitor student understanding over the duration of a unit of study that includes all three experiences. It is also beneficial to keep informal records during periods of observation (e.g., field trips). This information can be transferred to the rubric at a later time.

Make the Assignment

For an observation activity, take the class on a field trip and instruct students to make written notes or sketches of what they experience. They will use this written record later for a response extension activity, such as compiling a list of attractions at a local planetarium.

For an interview activity, instruct students to work in pairs to develop three to five questions they can ask each other that will provide important information. Questions should require more than a yes or no response. Then have students interview each other.

An activity for participation might be to assign students to pairs to participate in a field experience, such as a math measuring exercise or science experiment. Both members of the team should take an active role in the exercise.

Assess Student Understanding

Observation
■ uses notes as basis for creative response

Develop an activity that allows students to use the recorded notes, such as a brochure listing attractions at the field trip site. Review the list for accuracy.

FIRSTHAND EXPERIENCE

Task: Student will participate in experiences (field trip, interview, experiment) to gather information.

Goal/Standard: Participation meets stated criteria.

Criteria	2	1	0	Total Points
Observation (field trip)	Uses notes as basis for creative response	Observes presentation and takes notes	Fails to observe presentation	_____ x 3 = _____ points
Interview (expert on subject)	Asks subject 3 to 5 pertinent questions	Asks subject 3 to 5 random questions	Fails to conduct interview	_____ x 3 = _____ points
Participation (experiment or field trial)	Participates in experiment or field trial	Observes experiment or field trial	Fails to participate in experiment or field trial	_____ x 4 = _____ points

19–20 = A
18 = B
16–17 = C
14–15 = D
<14 = F

Total score _____/20 = _____

Interview

■ asks subject three to five pertinent questions

Students should be able to produce some evidence of the interview subject's responses, either a written or verbal account. Review the questions and responses, noting whether each question required more than a yes or no answer and whether the questions sought information that revealed more about the person than simply his or her favorite color or TV show.

Participation

■ participates in experiment or field trial

Because you will conduct this assessment during the experiment or field trial, keep the rubric at hand during those times. Note student cooperation and active participation in the experiment.

How to Use the

FIRSTHAND EXPERIENCE
Rubric

at the Intermediate Level

Introduce the Rubric

Distribute and discuss the rubric with students before they begin the assignment. Focus attention on the column containing the highest level of performance, reminding students that to receive full credit, they must achieve these objectives. This rubric is well suited for a science unit. Because it deals with three different types of firsthand experience—observation, interview, and participation—you need not complete the rubric at a single session but may use it to monitor student understanding over the duration of a unit of study that includes all three experiences. It is also beneficial to keep informal records during observation periods (e.g., field trips) that you can then transfer to the rubric at a more convenient time.

Make the Assignment

For an observation activity, instruct students to make notes and sketches during a field trip and then to use those tools to develop three or four questions relating to the experience.

For an interview, instruct students to develop three or four open-ended (requiring more than a yes or no response) questions before conducting an interview with an adult relative. Then have them use the interview subject's responses to develop three additional questions that occurred to them during the interview.

For a participation activity, instruct students to select an experiment in a content area subject to conduct for the class or for a small group of classmates.

Assess Student Understanding

Observation

- uses notes and observations to ask relevant questions

Review questions for relevance to student notes and field experience and require verbal clarification for vague responses.

RESEARCH **FIRSTHAND EXPERIENCE** INTERMEDIATE

Task: Student will participate in experiences (field trip, interview, experiment) to gather information.

Goal/Standard: Participation meets stated criteria.

Giving 0 points is an option—no evidence, no credit.

Criteria	4	3	2	1	Total Points
Observation (field trip)	Uses notes and observations to ask relevant questions	Records notes about experience	Observes presentation actively	Observes presentation satisfactorily	_____ x 3 = _____ points
Interview (expert on subject)	Uses subject's responses to formulate new questions	Asks subject 3 to 5 pertinent questions	Asks subject 3 to 5 random questions	Asks subject 1 or 2 random questions	_____ x 3 = _____ points
Participation (experiment or field trial)	Conducts experiment or field trial	Participates in experiment or field trial actively	Participates in experiment or field trial actively	Participates satisfactorily in experiment or field trial	_____ x 4 = _____ points

19–20 = A
18 = B
16–17 = C
14–15 = D
<14 = F

Total score _____/40 = _____

Interview

- uses subject's responses to formulate new questions

Review additional questions for relevance to interview subject's responses and require verbal clarification for vague responses.

Participation

- conducts experiment or field trial

Observe student-conducted experiment for student's ability to conduct the trial and convey information. The emphasis here is on getting students involved in the process, rather than insisting that they conduct an experiment or field trial that is a total success. The purpose of the rubric element is to get students out of their seats and actively participating.

How to Use the
WRITTEN REPORT Rubric
at the Intermediate Level

Introduce the Rubric

Distribute and discuss the rubric with students before they begin the assignment, focusing attention on the column containing the highest level of performance. Remind students that to receive full credit they must achieve these objectives.

Make the Assignment

Instruct students to select and get your approval on a topic question and write a report that answers the question by using available resources. The written report should be four to six pages long, excluding any illustrations or graphics, and the bibliography should have at least three entries. Remind students that they must not plagiarize, and require photocopies or computer printouts of sources with information they used highlighted. To ensure accuracy, you might limit choice of topics to those you have covered in the curriculum.

Assess Student Understanding

Topic
■ answers topic question adequately

Depth of Understanding
■ grasps concepts well

Accuracy
■ accurate information with complete documentation of accuracy

Bibliography
■ all accurate with appropriate dates

Determine whether students have addressed the topic question adequately. The report should reflect the student's grasp of concepts the report covers. The bibliography, with at least three entries, should contain accurate author names, titles, and publishing information. The bibliography should consist primarily of recent references (not older than 5 years), although a small number of older references is acceptable, depending on the topic. (A paper on Abraham Lincoln can use older references; a paper on the Internet cannot.)

WRITTEN REPORT

Task: Student will produce a written research project.

Goal/Standard: Project meets stated criteria.

Criteria	3	2	1	Total Points
Topic	Answers topic question adequately	Answers topic question but includes too much irrelevant material	Has minor gaps in answer to topic question	____ x 3 = ____ points
Depth of understanding	Grasps concepts well	Grasps concepts adequately	Grasps some concepts	____ x 4 = ____ points
Accuracy	Accurate information with complete documentation of accuracy	Accurate information, but incomplete documentation of accuracy	Errors in accuracy and incomplete documentation of accuracy	____ x 4 = ____ points
Bibliography	All accurate with appropriate dates	Accurate with some outdated references	Some inaccurate or outdated references	____ x 4 = ____ points

42–45 = A
39–41 = B
35–38 = C
32–34 = D
<32 = F

Total score ____/45 = ____

How to Use the
COLLABORATION Rubric
at the Intermediate Level

Introduce the Rubric

Distribute and discuss the rubric with students before they begin the assignment, focusing attention on the column containing the highest level of performance. Remind students that to receive full credit they must achieve these objectives.

Make the Assignment

Students can complete this assignment through a wide variety of group projects, ranging from a verbal in-class presentation to a writers' collaboration. The emphasis here is on student cooperation in a group. Although this rubric presumes students have some experience working in cooperative groups, you may want to review the rules of group work, including respecting others' opinions, waiting for a turn to speak, completing the task the group assigns them, and working as a unit to complete the project. Once they have the assignment, students need 3 to 5 days to complete the project.

Assess Student Understanding

Sharing Information
- shares information with all group members

Listening
- makes full eye contact with speaker; asks encouraging, open-ended questions

Nonverbal Communication
- exhibits encouraging, involved gestures and facial expressions

Division of Tasks

■ distributes tasks logically based on level of difficulty

Because you will conduct this assessment while observing students in the group setting, keep the rubric at hand during those times. Look for fair division of labor. For example, a student who takes on a particularly complex task should not take on a second task. Make notes about individual behaviors and overall group cooperation. Intervene only when the group's collapse seems inevitable. Otherwise, allow students to work through conflicts independently.

COLLABORATION

Task: Student will participate in a collaborative research project.

Goal/Standard: Participation meets stated criteria.

Criteria	4	3	2	1	Total Points
Sharing information	Shares information with all group members	Shares information with most group members	Shares information with a few group members	Shares minimal information	____ x 3 = ____ points
Listening	Makes full eye contact with speaker; asks encouraging, open-ended questions	Looks at speaker; asks relevant questions	Makes occasional eye contact with speaker; asks questions	Demonstrates adequate listening skills/ behaviors	____ x 4 = ____ points
Nonverbal communication	Exhibits encouraging, involved gestures and facial expressions	Exhibits supportive gestures and facial expressions	Exhibits positive gestures and facial expressions	Exhibits minimal gestures and facial expressions	____ x 4 = ____ points
Division of tasks	Distributes tasks logically based on level of difficulty	Distributes tasks based on time needed to complete them	Distributes tasks so that each group member has same number	Adequate distribution of tasks	____ x 4 = ____ points

56–60 = A
52–55 = B
47–51 = C
42–46 = D
<42 = F

Total score _____/60 = _____

Rubrics and Classroom Technology

8

Michael, an elementary school principal, is committed to finding ways of incorporating technology in the classroom. Although many of his students demonstrate a high level of proficiency with video games and other tasks, such as using educational software, Michael is concerned that they lack skills for such 21st-century tasks as developing multimedia presentations. Citing early exposure as a positive factor in developing students' technological expertise, Michael works with Guy, another principal, to design and implement a technology curriculum, including assessment rubrics to monitor student growth throughout the program.

EXPANDING TECHNOLOGY USE

Michael and Guy join other educators concerned about students' readiness to face the challenges of an increasingly tech-dependent society. The Internet is a massive clearinghouse of information accessible to those individuals with the ability to harness its resources. E-commerce and e-communication have proved to be more than a passing trend, and all students must learn to thrive in a world they can access from a desktop.

In addition to the Internet, recent advances in the fields of video and audio technology make these resources more student friendly. No longer limited to printed presentations, students can now share their ideas with others through sophisticated formats using multimedia and presentation software. These alternate avenues of self-expression can motivate even the most reluctant learner to become actively involved in the learning process. Increasing students' skills in technology in the classroom will strengthen their ability to succeed in a world that grows smaller with distant neighbors only a mouse click away. To that end, it is critical that students develop greater information literacy, demonstrating an ability to access, evaluate, and use information they acquire via the Internet as well as other more traditional resources.

The rubrics in this chapter cover the following technological areas: e-mail messages, video presentations, computer-generated multimedia presentations, and information literacy standards. The rubrics list full-credit responses to provide teachers with concrete examples of what they may see in student work. A summary of the expectations for the age and grade level follows. In cases when students in more than one grade level have all the skills described, the rubric and assessment guidelines have been combined. In the case of areas not suitable for primary grades, no rubric is provided.

E-MAIL MESSAGES

Electronic mail is a widely used method of communicating with people everywhere—whether they are next door or on the other side of the world. Because, in many instances, e-mail replaces telephone or face-to-face interaction, creating the proper tone in these messages is extremely important. The sender may not have the opportunity to clarify intent for the recipient, so the sender must pay special attention to phrasing. Students should develop the habit of rereading e-mail messages before sending them to make certain that the tone is positive, nonconfrontational, and appropriate, considering the sender's relationship (personal, professional) with the recipient. The rubric here applies to all levels and assesses students' ability to compose and send an e-mail message. The goal, or highest degree of accomplishment on the rubric, for primary as well as intermediate is as follows: Student uses correct address for recipient, uses appropriate greeting and closing in message, and composes message of appropriate, positive tone that is free of spelling and grammatical errors.

How to Use the
E-MAIL MESSAGE Rubric
at the Primary and Intermediate Levels

Introduce the Rubric

Distribute and discuss the rubric. Focus attention on the column containing the highest level of performance, reminding students that to receive full credit they must achieve these objectives.

Make the Assignment

Instruct students to compose and send an e-mail message to another individual. The person can be a friend, a relative, or a pen pal at another school. The message should be free of spelling and grammatical errors and the topic appropriate for the intended recipient. For example, if a student writes to a grandparent, the topic will differ from that of a message to a good friend. Because the recipient of an e-mail message cannot know the sender's mood from the printed word, users of e-mail communication must reread their messages before sending them and consider whether the recipient could perceive the tone as confrontational or argumentative.

Assess Student Understanding

Recipient Address
- present and correct

Greeting and Closing
- present and appropriate for recipient

Spelling and Grammar
- no errors

Tone of Message
- appropriate for recipient

TECHNOLOGY   # E-MAIL MESSAGE   PRIMARY AND INTERMEDIATE

Task: Student will compose and send an e-mail message.

Goal/Standard: Message meets stated criteria.

Criteria	2	1	0	Total Points
Recipient address	Present and correct	Present but incorrect	Not present	____ x 3 = ____ points
Greeting and closing	Present and appropriate for recipient	Present but inappropriate	Not present	____ x 4 = ____ points
Spelling and grammar	No errors	Few errors	Several errors	____ x 3 = ____ points
Tone of message	Appropriate for recipient	Inappropriate for recipient	Unclear	____ x 5 = ____ points

28–30 = A
26–27 = B
24–25 = C
21–23 = D
<21 = F

Total score ____ /30 = ____

Examine e-mail messages before students send them to check for spelling and grammatical errors as well as appropriateness of greeting, closing, and message topic. If any of these items requires revising, instruct students to make changes before they send the message.

VIDEO PRESENTATIONS: LIGHTS, CAMERA, ACTION

Although movies have been part of our culture for decades, student filmmaking is a relatively new venture. Video technology provides budding film artists with a number of user-friendly tools for telling stories, expressing opinions, or creating a visual poem to celebrate nature. These rubrics assess intermediate students' ability to produce a short (3–10 minute) video presentation with visual effects: The goal, or highest level of achievement, is as follows: Student produces video with a well-developed concept, logical sequence, seamless visual effects, and superior overall video quality.

How to Use the

VIDEO PRESENTATION
Rubric

at the Intermediate Level

Introduce the Rubric

Distribute and discuss the rubric beforehand, focusing attention on the column containing the highest level of performance. Remind students that to receive full credit they must achieve these objectives.

Make the Assignment

The increased availability of camcorders, digital cameras, and DVD hardware and software has made video a viable option for student response and self-expression. Students strong in visual-spatial intelligence often find this avenue more effective for conveying emotions or information to others. Instruct students to choose a topic. While students become acquainted with the film medium, it is best to provide a list of possible topics, such as "My Hero(ine)." You might also give students a topic from a content area, such as recycling, and encourage them to use video to share information they have gathered about it. Establish a time limit for the video production, 10 to 15 minutes for this grade level, and encourage students to look for images that will leave a lasting impression in the minds of viewers.

Assess Student Understanding

Concept Development
■ well-developed with scenes building on each other

Visual Effects
■ present and seamless

Overall Video Quality
■ superior

TECHNOLOGY · **VIDEO PRESENTATION** · INTERMEDIATE

Task: Student will produce a short (3–10 minutes) video presentation.

Goal/Standard: Video meets stated criteria.

Giving 0 points is an option—no evidence, no credit.

Criteria	4	3	2	1	Total Points
Concept development	Well developed with scenes building on each other	Well developed; good sequence	Adequate development; logical sequence	Underdeveloped or gaps in sequence	____ x 5 = ____ points
Visual effects	Present and seamless	Present and effective	Present and adequate	Present but distracting	____ x 5 = ____ points
Overall video quality	Superior	Excellent	Good	Fair	____ x 5 = ____ points

56–60 = A
52–55 = B
47–51 = C
42–46 = D
<42 = F

Total score ____/60 = ____

Reflect on the topics while reviewing the video. Think about how the student has conveyed information to viewers. Images should be effective and relevant to the main topic. Students should use visual effects, such as fade-in and fade-out, to enhance the production quality of the video. The sound and picture quality should be superior.

COMPUTER-GENERATED MULTIMEDIA PRESENTATIONS

Using computers to create multimedia presentations offers a powerful opportunity to both engage students at high levels and prepare them for their futures in a technologically advanced world. Reflecting on a much earlier invention, such as the calculator, illustrates the need for schools to tailor curriculum to meet future demands on learners. Presentation software, such as Microsoft's PowerPoint, is frequently used in college classrooms and in the business sector. This software enables users to develop and share a multimedia presentation. Provide students with an in-class introduction to the software and allow them to work in pairs or triads to develop skills before giving an assignment that will be assessed. The goal, or highest degree of accomplishment, for intermediate-level students on the rubric follows: Students will use presentation software to construct and share a multimedia presentation that includes a well-developed concept, follows a logical sequence, and demonstrates appropriate use of the software.

How to Use the

COMPUTER-GENERATED MULTIMEDIA PRESENTATION Rubric

at the Intermediate Level

Introduce the Rubric

Distribute and discuss the rubric beforehand, focusing attention on the column containing the highest level of performance. Remind students that to receive full credit they must achieve these objectives.

Make the Assignment

Instruct students to select a topic of importance to them (ecological conservation, pet care, etc.) and use presentation software to develop a multimedia presentation that presents their views on the topic. Depending on students' level of expertise with the software, teachers may wish to set a time limit or a specific number of images to be used in the presentation. Stress the importance of preventing the visual effects from overshadowing the impact of the message. A usable example might be a movie with outstanding special effects that fails to engage the audience in the story or characters. Effective use of any software is in harnessing it to enhance rather than detract from the presenter's message.

Assessing Student Understanding

Well-Developed Idea
- appropriate scope for topic
- idea appropriate for format

Logical Sequence
- clear opening, middle, and ending
- balance of major ideas and details

COMPUTER-GENERATED
MULTIMEDIA PRESENTATION

Task: Student will use presentation software to develop a multimedia presentation promoting an issue (i.e., ecological conservation).

Goal/Standard: Presentation will meet stated criteria.

Criteria	2	1	0	Total Points
Well-developed idea • appropriate scope for topic • idea appropriate for format	2 complete elements present	1 complete element present	Evidence of 1+ incomplete elements	____ x 3 = ____ points
Logical sequence • clear opening, middle, and ending • balance of major ideas and details	2 complete elements present	1 complete element present	Evidence of 1+ incomplete elements present	____ x 3 = ____ points
Appropriate use of software· • demonstrates ability to use software • appropriate design choices	2 complete elements present	1 complete element present	Evidence of 1+ incomplete elements	____ x 3 = ____ points

17–18 = A
15–16 = B
14 = C
13 = D
<13 = F

Total score ____/18 = ____

Appropriate Use of Software
- demonstrates ability to use software
- appropriate design choices

Take notes during the students' multimedia presentations, noting technical (design choices, ability to use software) and nontechnical (balance of major ideas or details, logical sequence) skills. A suggested modification for this rubric would be to weigh the elements evenly for the first assignment and, in later assignments, put greater weight on the technical elements to stress the importance of learning how to use the technology appropriately.

INFORMATION LITERACY SKILLS

The Chinese proverb states that teaching a person to fish feeds that person for a lifetime. Like this proverb, giving students the necessary tools for locating and using information enables them to become lifelong learners who are not forced to rely on a restricted amount of information provided for them by others. This life skill represents an invaluable component in students' critical thinking abilities because knowing how to access information independently empowers students to seek out answers to questions that arise in their daily lives. Information-literate individuals are not bound by hearsay or prepackaged sound bites that restrict the amount and nature of the information they require to make sound judgments. The goal, or highest degree of accomplishment on the rubric, for intermediate students follows: Students will demonstrate information literacy skills by using the Internet and other resources to develop and present a response to a predetermined question.

How to Use the

INFORMATION LITERACY Rubric

at the Intermediate Level

Introduce the Rubric

Distribute and discuss the rubric prior to beginning the assignment. Remind students that to receive full credit for their work they must meet the stated criteria for the highest level of understanding.

Make the Assignment

Begin with a classroom discussion about the types of questions, personal and universal, that arise for students in their day-to-day lives. What should students do when parents, guardians, teachers, or other adults are unable to provide sufficient answers? Introduce students to the various resources they can use to find their own answers to these questions. Next, work with students to develop a question that can be researched using these resources. On the first attempt, it may be advisable to allow students to work in pairs or triads on the assignment. On later assignments, students should work independently. Check with students to determine that the questions developed will work for this assignment. Avoid questions that have a simple yes-or-no or single-word answer. Use class examples of questions that require more in-depth research, such as "What causes pollution?" or "What can be done to improve our quality of air?" Set a specific time limit for students to locate information to respond to their questions. Do as much of this assignment as possible in the classroom so you can observe how students seek information.

Assessing Student Understanding

Accessing Information
- connects ideas to a central topic
- states more than one side of an issue
- locates information using a variety of formats

Students with less mature information literacy skills tend to gather information without finding a way to connect ideas to one another or to a central topic. They also tend to make no distinction between minor details and major ideas. Encourage students to use a webbing technique to list all information before identifying and developing links between specific items they have gathered.

TECHNOLOGY **INFORMATION LITERACY** INTERMEDIATE

Task: Student will use information resources to respond to a predetermined question.

Goal/Standard: Completed project will meet the stated criteria.

Criteria	4	3	2	1	Total Points
Accessing information • connects ideas to a central topic • states more than one side of an issue • locates information using a variety of formats	3 complete elements present	2 complete elements present	1 complete element present	Evidence of 2+ incomplete elements	_____ x 3 = _____ points
Evaluating information • identifies fact-based information • uses facts and opinions appropriately • identifies author bias	3 complete elements present	2 complete elements present	1 complete element present	Evidence of 2+ incomplete elements	_____ x 3 = _____ points
Using information • organizes information appropriately • develops problem-solving strategies • selects effective format for conveying information	3 complete elements present	2 complete elements present	1 complete element present	Evidence of 2+ incomplete elements	_____ x 3 = _____ points

33–36 = A
31–32 = B
28–30 = C
25–29 = D
<25 = F

Total score _____/36 = _____

Evaluating Information

- identifies fact-based information
- uses facts and opinions appropriately
- identifies author bias

A student possessing age- or grade-level appropriate information literacy skills is able to recognize the difference between a fact that can be substantiated with proof and the opinion of an individual who may be able to gain from promoting a particular theory (an individual who owns a business stating that items manufactured by that business are "the best" items available). Let students know that it is okay to include opinions in reports as long as they are clearly identified as opinion and that their source is noted to let readers know who feels that way.

Uses Information

- organizes information appropriately
- develops problem-solving strategies
- selects effective format for conveying information

Being able to acquire information is one of the major components of information literacy. Organizing and sharing information in the most appropriate format is another key component. Many learners are able to gather information but have difficulty conveying the information to others in a format that is easily understood. The type of information often dictates the way in which it is shared with others. Students working with gathered information may need to employ problem-solving skills to develop ways to share the information with others. This skill is at the heart of persuasive writing and speaking experiences because preparing information effectively results in a stronger impact on its reading or listening audience. At the conclusion of this assignment, instruct students to share their work with others in a written (report or pamphlet) or verbal (presentation or dialogue) mode.

Appendix: Internet Sites

RUBRIC-RELATED WEB SITES

All About Assessment and Rubrics: a collection of links to Web sites offering an introduction to rubrics, advice on creating them, and many sample rubrics to assess student writing

http://www.suelebeau.com/assessment.htm

Chicago Public Schools, Performance Assessment, Ideas and Rubrics: an introduction to assessment rubrics and tips on rubric construction

http://intranet.cps.k12.il.us/Assessments/Ideas_and_Rubrics/ideas_and_rubrics.html

Evaluation Rubrics for Websites: rubrics for students in primary, intermediate, and secondary grades to evaluate Web sites when conducting research on the Internet

http://www.siec.k12.in.us/~west/online/eval.htm

Exploring the Environment—Teacher Pages: an introduction to rubrics that includes a rationale for using assessment rubrics and advice on rubric construction

http://www.cotf.edu/ete/teacher/rubrics.html

Kathy Schrock's Guide for Educators—Assessment Rubrics: a categorized, annotated list of more than 1,600 sites to help educators, teachers, and parents enhance instruction and support the curriculum

http://school.discovery.com/schrockguide/assess.html

"Kid Language" Writing Rubrics: rubrics geared toward middle school students in the areas of writing to inform or persuade and for personal expression

http://www.intercom.net/local/school/sdms/mspap/kidwrit.html

National Reading Panel: online compilation of work completed and articles relating to this panel; includes information regarding the education law No Child Left Behind Act

http://www.nationalreadingpanel.org

Rubric Sampler—Relearning by Design: provides practical examples and guidelines for building and adjusting rubrics for specific learning situations

http://www.relearning.org/resources/PDF/rubric_sampler.pdf

Rubrics for Web Lessons: a case for using rubrics in authentic assessment, links to articles about rubrics and authentic assessment, holistic rubrics for various topics, a rubric template, and other rubric resources

http://webquest.sdsu.edu/rubrics/weblessons.htm

Teacher Vision–comprehensive online collection of resources for teachers, including a significant section on rubrics assessment that discusses its present applications and future uses; also contains some links to sites that offer teachers assistance in constructing specific rubrics for their own classrooms

http://www.teachervision.com

Teachnology: Handy site with rubric generators—you plug in the type of rubric you want, and it generates a rubric for you, personalized with the school and teacher name; generators in all major content areas and some unique areas as well

http://www.bestteachersites.com/web_tools/rubrics/

"Understanding Rubrics": an article (originally published in *Educational Leadership*) on rubrics, their use, and their design; features tips for creating rubrics and examples of analytic rubrics for such areas as book reports, oral presentations, persuasive essays, and more

http://www.middleweb.com/rubricsHG.html

GENERAL, USEFUL WEB SITES FOR TEACHERS

AskScott

http://www.askscott.com/

Education World—The Educator's Best Friend
http://www.education-world.com/

Inki & Taz's Poetry Corner
http://library.thinkquest.org/11883/

Kathy Schrock's Guide for Educators
http://school.discovery.com/schrockguide/

Teachers Helping Teachers
http://www.pacificnet.net/~mandel/

Teachers.Net
http://www.teachers.net/

Teachnet.com
http://www.teachnet.com/

Bibliography

Arter, J., & McTighe, J. (2000). *Scoring rubrics in the classroom: Using performance criteria for assessing and improving student performance.* Thousand Oaks, CA: Corwin Press.

Beamon, G. (2001). *Teaching with adolescent learning in mind.* Thousand Oaks, CA: Corwin Press.

Burke, K. (2006). *From standards to rubrics in 6 steps.* Thousand Oaks, CA: Corwin Press.

Burke, K., Fogarty, R., & Belgrad, S. (2002). *The portfolio connection: Student work linked to standards* (2nd ed.). Thousand Oaks, CA: Corwin Press.

Carlson, A. (2002). *Authentic learning: What does it really mean?* Bellingham: Western Washington University. Retrieved May 8, 2006, fromhttp://pandora.cii.wwu.edu/showcase2001/authentic_learning.htm

Depka, E. (2001). *Designing rubrics for mathematics.* Thousand Oaks, CA: Corwin Press.

Georgia Educational Technology Training Center. (2001). *Assessment rubrics.* Retrieved May 8, 2006, from http://edtech.kennesaw.edu/intech/rubrics.htm

Glasgow, J. (Ed.). (2002). *Standards-based activities with scoring rubrics: Middle and high school English: Volume 1: Portfolios.* Larchmont, NY: Eye on Education.

Gronlund, N. (1998). *Assessment of student achievement* (6th ed.). Needham Heights, MA: Allyn & Bacon.

Huck, C., Hepler, S., Hickman, J., & Keifer, B. (2004). *Huck's children's literature in the elementary school* (8th ed.). New York: McGraw-Hill.

McMillan, J. H. (2001). *Classroom assessment: Principles and practice for effective instruction.* Needham Heights, MA: Allyn & Bacon.

Mertler, C. (2001). Designing scoring rubrics for your classroom. Practical assessment, research, and evaluation. *Education Update, 7*(25). Retrieved May, 8, 2006, from http://PAREonline.net/getvn.asp?v=7&n=25

Miller, W. H. (2001). *Alternative assessment techniques for reading and writing.* San Francisco: Jossey-Bass.

National Institute of Child Health and Human Development. (2000). *Report of the National Reading Panel: Teaching children to read: An evidence-based assessment of the scientific research literature on reading and its implications for reading instruction* (NIH Publication No. 00–4769). Washington, DC: U.S. Government Printing Office.

Olson, C. B. (2002). *The reading/writing connection: Strategies for teaching and learning in the secondary classroom.* Needham Heights, MA: Allyn & Bacon.

Olson, L. (2002). Up close and personal. *Education Week, 21*(37), 28–33.

O'Neil, J. (1996). Teaching for performance: New assessments help reshape classroom practice, *Education Update, 38*(8). Retrieved May 10, 2006, from http://www.ascd.org/portal/site/ascd/menuitem.c97770c239d90bdeb85516f762108a0c/

Opitz, M. F., & Ford, M. P. (2001). *Reaching readers: Flexible and innovative strategies for guided reading.* Portsmouth, NH: Heinemann.

Popham, W. J. (2005). *Classroom assessment: What teachers need to know* (4th ed.). Boston, MA: Allyn & Bacon.

Pressley, M. (2005). *Reading instruction that works* (3rd ed.). New York: Guilford Press.

Readence, J. E., Bean, T. W., & Baldwin, R. S. (2004). *Content area literacy: An integrated approach* (8th ed.). Dubuque, IA: Kendall/Hunt.

Schommer, M. (1995). Voices in education on authentic assessment. *Mid-western Educational Researcher, 8*(2), 13–14.

Sejnost, R., & Thiese, S. (2006). *Reading and writing across content areas* (2nd ed.). Thousand Oaks, CA: Corwin Press.

Sheffield-Gibbons, K. (2001). *The teacher's right hand: A resource guide of reading and writing strategies, lesson plans, and rubrics.* Bloomington, IN: 1st Books Library.

Spandel, V. (2001). *Books, lessons, ideas for teaching the six traits.* Boston, MA: Houghton Mifflin.

Spandel, V. (2005). *The 9 rights of every writer.* Portsmouth, NH: Heinemann.

Stauffer, R. (1969). *Teaching reading as a thinking process.* New York: Harper & Row.

Stiggins, R. J. (2004.) *Student-involved assessment for learning* (4th ed.). Upper Saddle River, NJ: Prentice Hall.

Vacca, R. T., & Vacca, J. L. (2005). *Content area reading: Literacy and learning across the curriculum* (8th ed.). Needham Heights, MA: Allyn & Bacon.

Index

CORWIN PRESS